My Summer with T-bone

By
Gus Brackett

Illustrations by
Belle Brackett

Twelve Baskets Book Publishing
Three Creek, Idaho

Twelve Baskets Book Publishing, LLC
54899 Crawfish Rd.
Rogerson ID 83302
www.badgerthurston.com
12bookbaskets@gmail.com

ISBN 9798844343391

Illustrations by Belle Brackett
Author photo by Jill Davidson, Emotion Portrait Design

Other books by Gus Brackett:
Badger Thurston and the Cattle Drive
Badger Thurston and the Runaway Stagecoach
Badger Thurston and the Mud Pits
Badger Thurston and the Trouble at the Rodeo
Nettie McCorkle and the Horse Race

Table of Contents

Acknowledgement

--To my family…stop trying to figure out which character is you. This is a work of fiction existing only in my demented imagination. You are not the subject of this—let me repeat—fictional account

Chapter One
In the beginning...

I'm a ranch kid. Being a ranch kid affects every part of my life. It affects the way I dress. I always wear cowboy boots. I can tie a honda on a lariat, I can tie a hangman's noose, a bow line knot, a baler knot, and an Alomar knot…but I can't tie my own shoes. I don't get enough practice. My Mom bought me a pair of shoes because my teacher insisted. I need shoes for PE, but I was always tripping on my laces so it made more sense to wear my cowboy boots. Besides that, I'm faster in my boots…it's because I have high arches. All cowboys have high arches.

I have two cowboy hats…my going to church hat and my everyday hat. I have to guard my everyday hat from my Mom. She wants to throw it away. It's a brown hat with a single crease in the center. There is a small hole in the front and a blackish tint in the crease that could only be described as grime. My Dad says that I can wear it as long as I don't mind looking like a hillbilly. The hillbilly look is what I'm shootin' for. Dad tells me you can wear a hat until it starts to stink. Then you have to throw it out.

Being a ranch kid doesn't just affect what I wear though. It affects every part of my life. For instance, we have television, but the reception is terrible. We get channel 6, channel 7, and channel 11. Channel 6 never comes in consistently enough to get through a show. Channel 11 only has shows for old people…and even when they have a show worth watching, there's always a ribbon of fuzz through the screen. It'll make you go cross-eyed after about an hour of watchin'.

So channel 7 is what we watch. The programming is fairly consistent. News in the morning, then game shows, followed by talk shows and the soap operas. My Mom's favorite is "Days of Our Lives." She always has "Days of Our Lives" on when it comes on, but I've never seen her stop to watch it. After the soaps is more talk shows, followed by more news and then you're into prime time. There's a couple hours of funny shows followed by an hour of a serious show and then the news again. The news hasn't changed at all in the last four hours, but to be sufficiently informed, you have to watch the news at both six and ten. After the news is Johnny Carson with the Late Show following that. But I better be in bed before the news at ten. After the Late Show, they play the national anthem, and you get either color bars or fuzz for the rest of the night.

Fuzz on my television really is my biggest struggle in life. I could live a normal life, watching TV like every other kid if it wasn't for the static on our TV. Any time an electrical appliance is working at our house, then the TV isn't working.

When Mom uses the blender, mixer, dishwasher, washing machine, or any other device that the modern house wife uses throughout the day and late into the night, then we can't watch TV.

It's the worst on Saturday morning. Saturday morning is a literal gold mine of kid programming. The cartoons come on right after the national anthem at 6:00 in the morning and there are cartoons until ten. But Saturday morning is when Mom does a full cleaning on the house. She will fire up the vacuum cleaner and vacuum every room in the house. And the TV is functionally dead until she finishes.

So we have to do other things. In the winter, we will do a lot of sledding. We will ride horses or bicycles. But in the spring, through the summer, and until Labor Day, our activities revolve around 4-H.

For those who are unfamiliar with 4-H, it is a nationwide youth organization that develops a child's hands, head, health, and heart, or the four H's of good living. In the city, 4-H can be a project of rocketry, cooking, bicycle, rabbits, government, or any number of projects to choose from.

But where I'm from, 4-H means a show steer. Technically, the project is called Market Beef. This project is actually quite an undertaking. You start with a 600-pound steer, and then feed it for two hundred days to at least one thousand pounds. The project culminates at our county fair with a couple of shows, a fat stock sale, and a thousand-dollar paycheck…which is a small fortune for a kid.

Every year, around the middle of February, the cold breaks, the snow melts enough to be muddy, and it's time to pick show steers. This is where I first meet T-bone. This is my first year taking a show steer to the fair. I'm familiar with the process though…I come from a big family…six kids in all. I have two older brothers and an older sister that started taking steers six years ago. Dad will sort out about twelve steers at weaning and put them in a pen with some smaller calves, sick calves, and maybe one or two with a bad leg. He feeds these calves more, so the steers that are in the prospects pen get fed a little bit more than everything else. So I get to choose one from these steers to be mine.

I don't really know what I'm looking for. I like the Herefords…those are the ones with red hair except on their feet and faces. Dad likes the black ones with a little bit of white on their faces. But he also tells me you shouldn't pick a steer based on its hair color. He says that, but If they have brown hair, or are completely white they won't even make it into the prospects pen. "Judges don't like white or brown," he says, "but don't pick a steer based on its hair color." It's all very confusing. So you want them to have a big butt. There's a lot of meat there. And you want them to be long. The longer they are the more steaks they make. It's no good if they're too short, and they can't be too tall…they have to be just right and I don't know what just right looks like. To tell you the truth, I don't think Dad really knows what just right looks like either.

Temperament is important too. Temperament just means how nice they are. We raise range cattle so all of our steers start out with a bad temperament. They aren't used to being around people, and they get nervous in tight spaces. For the first time in their lives, they are in a tight space with a lot of people around. So all of the steers in the prospects pen are a little bit crazy. Dad says some of them are just scared and will get over that with a little work and a little time. But others are just mean. And the best way to know the difference between the scared ones and the mean ones is…actually I can't tell the difference. But Dad knows the difference. When the scared ones look at him, he barely moves. When the mean steers look his way, he grabs onto the fence and sometimes puts one foot on the fence to climb it if the steer charges at him. The mean steers generally end up with bloody noses from running into fences.

Because I'm not very good at looking at steers, I'm going to pick my steer based on temperament and color. There are seven of the twelve that stand calmly and don't have bloody noses. Two of the steers are completely black, three are black with white faces, and two are Herefords. One of the Herefords has a big splotch of red on his white face that looks like South America. The other Hereford has the prettiest white face and curly hair on him.

"I want that one," I proclaim to the world. Everyone looks at me, pointing at my steer.

"What's his number?" my Dad asks. "I'll write him down as yours."

I squint my eyes and focus on the yellow ear tag with black numbers. The numbers are big enough to be seen, but too small to be seen easily. I stretch my neck and focus my eyes on the tag.

"The first number is seven," Dad says, "all of them this year start with a seven. I just need the last two numbers."

My Dad can see a baby calf hiding under a sagebrush two miles away. But he has to wear glasses to see words on a page right under his nose.

"Seven…eighty-one," I say.

"It's thirty-one, stupid," my sister Laney yells at me. She's fourteen so she communicates primarily through a series of emotional yelling. "What, are you blind?" My Dad is used to the yelling, but it sets my nerves on edge.

"Seven thirty-one," I tell my Dad.

"Seven thirty-one it is," my Dad repeats as he writes my name and the number in a small leather bound notebook/calendar that fits in his shirt pocket.

"Do you have a name picked out?" Dad asks.

"T-bone," I say proudly.

"T-bone?" my Dad questions. "Not T-rex or T-bird."

"T-bone," I say confidently so everyone knows not to bother talking me out of it.

"T-bone is the stupidest name I've ever heard," Laney yells. I shudder at the volume of her voice.

"Yeah, I'd stick with Seven thirty-one," my brother Jerry adds, "It's better than T-bone." Usually Jerry is pretty funny, but other times he just thinks he's funny. This is one of the other times.

"Quit messin' with your brother," my Dad is slightly agitated. With six of us kids, I'm surprised he's not agitated all of the time.

"So tell me Max, why T-bone."

"Well that's a whole 'nother story," I say. In fact, it's a story for chapter two.

Chapter Two
The Ecology of
Predator and Prey

Sunday nights are always a treat at the Hackberry household. Sunday is the day of rest. So that means waking up at 6:00 in the morning to get dressed up in church clothes, drive an hour and a half to church where you spend two hours trying to stay awake. Following church is a couple more hours of lunch and fellowship…fellowship is what church people call sitting around and gossiping. After that is an hour and a half drive home. When we get home, everyone is so tired from resting, that we all take a nap. Dinner is usually something simple like finger foods or popcorn.

But because Mom is so tired, she isn't running anything. The dish washer is silent, the washing machine sits empty, the vacuum cleaner is neatly stowed in the closet. She won't even turn on the stove to cook a meal. As you recall, the enemy of television is an appliance…but with all the appliances inactive, we actually could watch TV on Sunday night.

The highlight of Sunday evening programming on Channel seven is, and you have to say it in a deep, Mr. Announcer-guy voice, "Mutual of Omaha's Wild Kingdom." The host of the show was a stodgy, old British guy with a bad white mustache. He is ironically dressed in a khaki shirt, khaki shorts with black shoes and tall black socks. If he was a tourist, you'd call him a goober, but he is an adventurer so the fashion works.

In a thick British voice, he would say, "Out on the plains of the Sarengheti," I don't know where the Sarengheti is, but it was the epitome of wild animal, "roams the massive cheetah. The cheetah is the fastest animal on the plain. With razor sharp teeth and speeds reaching sixty miles per hour, the cheetah is the most feared predator on the Sarengheti." At this point the camera would pan to a family of cheetahs, usually doing nothing more than sleeping. Occasionally they would do something exciting like yawn. The diurnal activities of the cheetah are not overly dramatic.

The British narrator would then say, "Just down the savannah roams a small herd of gazelle." He may have said antelope, but gazelle sounds much more exotic. "The gazelles browse lazily on the small brush native to Central Africa."

This was all, believe it or not, very exciting to a kid a million miles away from Africa. It was sheer magic that brought these images of the African savannah into my home in Idaho. But the lesson I learned about wild animals were very relevant.

"Wild Kingdom" was usually pretty boring. I mean, how many different angles of a cheetah sleeping and yawning or a gazelle eating can you watch in an hour-long program. But at the end, our patience and perseverance is always rewarded. Dinner time for a cheetah involves a short search for the gazelles that we have been forced to watch graze for the last thirty-five minutes. In a flash, the cheetah pounces at an unsuspecting gazelle. The gazelle, less than enthusiastic about a dinner party with the cheetah, takes off at a run. The camera follows this intense race as good as it can.

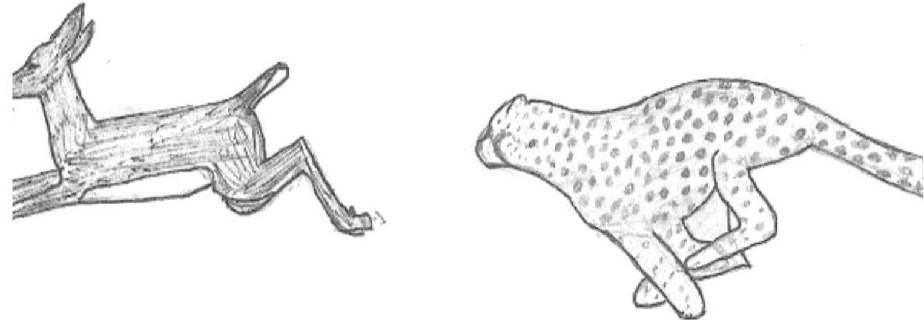

The narrator comes back, "This life and death struggle has a winner and a loser with every race. If the cheetah loses, he will face death from starvation. If the gazelle loses…," and at that point, the cheetah pounces on the gazelle and drags it to the ground. The gazelle is quickly torn to shreds as the cheetah feasts on his catch. "Mutual of Omaha's Wild Kingdom" would end with the cheetah enjoying his bloody meal.

The narrator wraps up the program with a final philosophical comment, "The drama of predator and prey plays out on a daily basis here on the Sarengheti. Tonight, the predator won the race…but the constant struggle between the hunger of the predator and the fear of the prey creates a perfect balance in the unrelenting ecosystem of the African plain." Bum-Bum-Bum Bummm, Bum, Bum-Bum-Bum-Bum Bud Dum Bum…That's the horns and strings playing the theme song as the ending credits roll and my Sunday night comes to an end.

Predator and Prey…it is a concept introduced to me on "Wild Kingdom," but there are deep seated tendencies of predators and prey even with domesticated animals like people and steers. Predators and prey have an interesting relationship. Prey have magical abilities to convert abundant materials like grass, flowers, and leaves into nutritious food for themselves. And predators have the magical ability to catch prey and eat the converted forage for their own nutrition.

Predators are animals that are at the top of the food chain. Predators have eyes in the front of their head and very keen vision. They have sharp front teeth and strong jaws. Most have sharp claws or talons and soft paws. They are very flexible and athletic, which enables them to stalk their meal. Even their digestive systems are designed to digest a high protein diet…mostly meat.

Humans are predators. So are wolves, mountain lions, bobcats, and a variety of animals with sharp teeth and claws.

Predators live their life based on hunger. Predators will kill, eat, and then have to kill again as their hunger drives them.

Prey, on the other hand, live their life driven by fear. In a world of predators and prey, the prey is always cautious and lives their life in fear of anything that might eat them. Prey have eyes in the side of their head. They are able to easily see all around them. Prey have huge stomachs and are able to convert abundant grass, flowers, and leaves into useable food…for predators. Their ultimate role in the ecosystem is to be a meal for a predator or a scavenger. And again, it is the same for domesticated animals. Cows, sheep, and pigs are all prey and are all destined to be a meal. These animals live their lives in fear of being eaten.

As humans, it is difficult to relate to either predators or prey. We have an abundance of food, so we don't really know hunger. Sure, we get hungry, but not the type of hunger that would make us run down an animal and bite into it while it is still alive. And with our prominent position on the food chain, we don't wake up every morning in imminent danger of being eaten.

That's how prey live every day of their lives. They know that their ultimate destiny is to be eaten…they live their life in fear to postpone that meal with a predator as long as they can.

The whole relationship between predators and prey is where I came up with the name T-bone. It all started with my dad explaining how the beef industry works. We spend nearly every waking hour doing what we can to keep our cows and calves alive. Then we sell them to a nice man down in the valley who slaughters them and cuts them into meat.

I like cows, calves, steers, and heifers. And I like a hamburger, steaks, roast beef and barbeque ribs. But I'm not completely comfortable with the process of turning steers and heifers into hamburgers, steak, and other meat products. Dad says most people other than the butcher aren't really comfortable with the process either…but most everyone is comfortable with the outcome.

My Dad is very up front when it comes to our show steers, "I want you know that these steers are not pets," My Dad tells me. "If you want to take a steer to the fair, you will sell him and he will go to the butcher." My Dad has a super serious voice that he uses in these situations.

"I know, Dad," I respond. I try using my super serious voice, but my voice isn't deep enough to be taken seriously…much less super seriously.

"You know that someday, your steer calf will be on somebody's plate as a hamburger or a T-bone steak," My Dad tells me.

So to prove to him that I was listening, I named my steer T-bone.

At this point in my project, it's really pretty boring. T-bone is about 700 pounds and over the next eight months, he needs to gain at least another 300 pounds to qualify for the fair. If he doesn't "make weight," then he won't sell and I don't get paid. The fair, and more importantly the sale, is the whole point of the project.

So at this point, all I have to do is feed my steer. I have to wake up fifteen minutes early, and trudge down to the barn. T-bone and the five other steers line up at the feed bunk eagerly awaiting their breakfast. My older brother Jerry pours a bag of grain into their feed bunk and me, Laney and Jimmy use pitchforks to fork hay to the steers.

Once the grain is in the feed trough, the steers push their way in and eat quickly. They root and slurp like a drove of pigs. The steers feed trough looks a lot like our dinner table. With six kids, you have to eat fast or you won't get your fair share.

I like watching T-bone eat. He pulls his ears back and wags his tail like a puppy. Mom says that each steer has its own personality. Dad always gets mad when Mom talks about a steer's personality.

"Steers aren't people," my Dad says.

Dad says we shouldn't anthropomorphize our steers. You don't know what anthropomorphize means…neither did I. Anthropomorphize means that you give an animal human characteristics. If you watch a movie and that animal speaks English, that is anthropomorphizing that animal. Or if you assume an animal has human emotions like love, sadness, envy or other emotions that come from the part of the brain that animals don't have.

So a steer doesn't have personality, but they have bovine-ality; a cow is a bovine, so bovine-ality. A horse has equine-ality, a dog has canine-ality, and a cat has feline-ality…because we all know a cat doesn't have any personality.

Dad says it is unfair to hold an animal to the high standard of personality. A steer will slobber all over you. They pee on your shoe and wait to fart until you are directly behind them. Steers have no manners; they are uncoordinated and knock you over. They kick, they butt you, and are the most selfish creatures alive. They don't listen and they never have a good word to say. If steers are judged by their personality, you would say they have a bad personality.

But amongst steers, they are all different and express themselves uniquely based on the limited emotions they possess. They each have unique bovine-ality. Some are mean and will run you up the fence. Dad says those don't make good show steers…but they hang just fine. Others are pretty friendly. Some are just kind of there.

T-bone has a good bovine-ality. His antics make me laugh. If I scratch him on the tail head, his whole butt wiggles.

I like to watch him eat. He is a total mess. He eats like the cookie monster, with grain spilling out of the sides of his mouth. And he is starting to get fat…which always reminds me of a steer's ultimate purpose.

Cattle are just like all prey. They will live a mundane life of eating as much as they can…and then they will get eaten. That is the purpose of cattle. I try not to dwell on the fact, but it's in the back of my mind.

It's important for me to remember the whole point of this project. I will care for T-bone, feed him, make him comfortable, and then sell him…and then T-bone will go on to cure world hunger. Or at least satisfy the craving of a cranky three-year-old with a happy meal hamburger. That's the whole point of a show steer. I'm the predator and T-bone is the prey.

Chapter Three
Wild Animal Trainer

Every spring my Mom takes all of us kids to the circus. The Shriners Family Circus sets up a tent with three rings at the county fairgrounds. Dad is always busy, or so he says. I think he just hates the circus.

I am always amazed by the acrobats. I get nervous watching the trapeze artists swinging back and forth in the rafters of the circus tent. I get anxious about the tight rope walkers. All of those flips and tumbles on that thin wire. I usually get a crook in my neck looking up at the acts.

But the real highlight is the wild animal tamers. The snake handlers don't impress me much, anybody that handles any reptiles on purpose is a little creepy to me. The cat tamers are very impressive in my mind. They courageously enter the center ring with a whip and a shield…usually a chair. But I think it's all for show. I mean, if the cats were really hungry or ferocious, they have over 500 meals to choose from sitting in the audience.

Now the elephant tamer, those are the most impressive to me. Anybody that can get a ton of anything to do what they want has my admiration. They don't use ropes or whips, usually just a little stick or quirt. The trainer will use subtle cues to get the elephant to perform feats of athleticism from these massive animals. It seems their only tool is the trust that has developed between the trainer and the elephant.

Maybe the reason I like the elephant trainer so much is because I can really relate to their work. Elephants are bigger than steers, but elephant trainers are bigger than 12-year-old boys. Either way, there is no way to manhandle either. For both, you have to use your ability to reason and knowledge of the species to get them to do what you want. But the elephant trainer has the advantage of experience. He's been working with elephants for decades. I've been working with my steer for about a month now.

I know that cattle are not wild animals. They have been domesticated for a couple of millennium now. Domesticated just means that people as a species owned them for a very long time. But a domesticated steer still doesn't want to be eaten, so they will run away if they can. And if they can't, they will kick, charge, butt, gore, stomp or do anything to keep a predator away.

We put T-bone into a small corral, so he can't run away. My dad puts a halter on him and has tied the lead rope to a fence. His only tools of resistance are to kick, charge, butt, gore or stomp me. And I really don't feel like getting kicked, charged, butted, gored, or stomped. But T-bone has to be tamed and it is my job to tame him.

T-bone has been tied up to the fence by his halter for about a half-hour now.

"Let the fence post soften him up a little bit," my Dad sagiously says. "There's no point in getting' beat up."

I think my Dad is just trying to help, but talk like that does little to ease my fear of getting kicked.

"Let's get in there and get hands on 'em," my Dad finally says.

Jerry, Laney and Jimmy climb off the fence they've been sitting on. They have done this before, so they walk right up to their steer and start petting them on the back. They evidently know where the magic spot is because they touch their steers and they instantly calm down and enjoy the massage.

I walk to a point near T-bone's shoulder, but at a point I'm sure he can't kick me. I reach out my hand as far as I can, but I'm several feet away from touching him. I tiptoe forward and reach a tipping point that makes T-bone freak out. He jumps his front feet off the ground and then pulls back hard on the rope. The rope tightens around his face. His face looks like mine when I put my palm on my face next to my ears and push my cheeks forward. "Look everybody, I'm chubby," I usually say. Everyone gets a great laugh, except for Mom who can't show any approval for such silliness. T-bone strains against the fence with his uncomfortable looking chubby face.

"You've gotta stand closer, Max." my Dad says.

"Like where?" I ask, hoping my Dad will just come up and do it.

"Take two steps forward," my Dad says. He's starting to use his whiny, I'm-getting-annoyed voice.

I take two microscopic, imperceptible shuffles forward. "Like this," I reply, using my whiny I-don't-care that-you're-getting-annoyed voice.

My Dad rolls his eyes and walks over to T-bone. He walks slowly but purposefully.

If T-bone could talk, he would be saying, "Don't eat me…don't eat me," over and over again in his pathetic little steer voice.

My Dad, ignoring T-bones imaginary pleas, reaches out and places his hand on T-bones side. Dad takes one more step and leans against my steer.

"You've gotta get in close to him," Dad says. "He can't kick you very hard if you're in close."

He can't kick me at all if I stand out of reach, I think to myself. I chuckle at my wit. Sometimes my little quips and back talking is funnier if I keep it to myself.

"Get in there and touch your steer, you big weanie," Laney yells at me.

"Your sister is right," Dad says, "even if her volume is a little too loud for the steer pen," Dad glares at Laney. "Come in here and touch him."

With my Dad shielding T-bone, I step up next to him and put my hand on T-bone.

"Talk to him," my Dad says.

"What should I say?" I ask.

"It doesn't matter…he's a steer."

"Hey, T-bone," I say, "I'm not gonna eat you,"

"Yet," my Dad adds with a smile.

He gets mad when I crack jokes at bad times, but it's okay for him. T-bone is startled and steps on my Dad's foot. He doesn't wince or cry out; he just pushes T-bone off and keeps petting him. I'm not sure what Dad's boots are made of, but I need to get a pair.

"Scratch him in between his shoulder blades," Dad tells me.

My hand slowly crawls up T-bones side until I'm scratching in between T-bones shoulder blades. Instantly T-bone relaxes. T-bone goes from, "Don't eat me…don't eat me," to "Oh yeah, right there…that's the spot." T-bone's ears drop and his tail wags easily. He enjoys the scratching between his shoulder blades.

At the same time, Dad scratches T-bone on the tail head. He scratches T-bone on the left side of his tail head and T-bone leans his whole back side to the left. Dad scratches T-bone on the right side and T-bone leans his backside to the right. T-bone relaxes completely and enjoys the massage.

"So there is a magic spot that make this easy," I tell my Dad.

"There's several magic spots," my Dad says without stopping. "They like it down low." My Dad reaches between T-bone's hind legs and scratches T-bone's cod. T-bone's ears drop and his tail wags. He lifts up his left hind leg and shakes it in rhythm with the scratching like a dog when he's scratched on the belly.

"Just like a puppy," I say.

"Yep, just like a puppy."

I reach forward to scratch T-bone behind his ears just like our dog likes. I barely touch him and he freaks out. He stomps and pulls violently against his halter.

"Don't touch his head," My Dad yells louder than necessary.

"I'm sorry," I say, "I didn't know…"

"You don't have to be sorry, you just need to know," my Dad calms his voice. As I step back, T-bone calms down as quickly as Dad did and looks back for the good scratching to continue.

"How long do I need to pet him?" I ask, hoping it's not long.

"The more time you put into him, the better he'll be," my dad replies.

Another thirty seconds, I think to myself. I know better than to say that out loud. Everyone else stops first so I step back and let T-bone relax. My Dad walks around and unties all of the steers. It amazes me how he slides right up to the steer and does what he needs to. He gets stepped on and it's no big deal. He gets kicked by the steer and he doesn't yell out or scream. My Dad's not tough like a middle linebacker or a bull rider, but he is tough. Actually, upon further reflection, I don't really think my Dad is that tough. I think he's just stubborn. He'll stubbornly stand too close to a steer, or stand his ground when less stubborn people, or less tough, would move.

It also amazes me how fast a steer goes back to being a steer. They buck and kick. The steers fight and play with each other just after their liberation. It's like they're celebrating an encounter with a predator without being eaten. Steers are just funny that way.

The next step in getting a steer trained is to teach them to lead. When you think about leading a steer, just picture an 800-pound steer, in a tug of war with a 110-pound boy. It's really not much of a match. The steer wins every time. Even my Dad has trouble getting them to lead…and he has four children with steers, so he would have to lead four steers. It's not a job he has even considered doing.

Instead, we give them what is referred to as the "Massey" treatment. Now the Massey treatment is not painful, and it takes no special technical skill. It's really quite simple.

To understand the Massey treatment, you first need to know what a Massey is. It is a small tractor. The Massey is a 1952 Massey-Ferguson 10 horse power tractor. It's small…really too small to do much ranch work, so it is usually available for the Massey treatment. It has a gas engine that pops and backfires and makes all kinds of noise…which is an integral part of the Massey treatment.

The Massey has a bar attached to the three-point hitch called a draw bar. Four steers can be tied to the draw bar and the draw bar can be raised to about the level of a child.

The steers are tied to the Massey and Dad fires the tractor up…or at least tries to. It cranks and sputters and pops, but doesn't start. The steers twist anxiously at the end of their ropes.

"What are we waiting for?" Laney yells. "I don't have all afternoon."

My Dad looks up and starts to speak, but he chokes on his words. Apparently, it's just not worth the fight.

My Dad finds a screw driver in a box of the tractor. He fiddles with a bulb and squirts some starter fluid in the air intake. He presses the start button and this time the tractor fires up.

Chug-a-chug-a-pop-pop,   chug-a –chug-a-pop-pop. The Massey is loud and belches black smoke from the pipe on the top of the hood. The steers are disturbed by this mysterious piece of equipment. Dad jumps on the tractor and throttles it up.

"Wasp clorn na stees," I hear my Dad tell me. I'm not sure that I heard him right.

"What?" I yell back, making every effort not to sound annoyed.

"Walk close to the steers," my Dad yells back, making no effort to hide his annoyance. I step close, but not too close to T-bone.

Dad pushes the clutch in and grinds the tractor into gear. He lifts his foot off the clutch and the Massey lurches forward. All of the halters pull tight and all of the steers reluctantly step forward. The rope pulls tight again and the steers take another step in unison. For the first ten steps, they perform this yank-step, two step with the tractor. Then they figure it out and walk dutifully behind the Massey.

If at any point the steers object to walking, the lead rope pulls tight and the mighty little tractor drags the steers to another step. The steers concede that resistance is futile.

I really like the Massey treatment. I don't know why. It's too loud to talk. And maybe that's it…it's too loud to hear Laney yelling at me. And it's too loud to hear Jerry making jokes about me. But I don't think that's it. I just get to walk next to my Dad and we get our work done together.

It's not enough just to train your steer. You also have to train their hair. My Mom grew up in the city, so there are some things that country folk do that is just plain silly. Don't get me wrong, she's very supportive and appreciates the importance of showing steers, but some of the stuff we see as critically important, she sees as weird.

My Mom says that a steer show is the same thing as a beauty pageant. We put our steers on a special diet, except to make them fat, not skinny. The last thing we do is style their hair. We wash their hair, comb it, add special conditioner to make it grow long, and then spend a few days before the fair to trim it up neat. About the only thing we don't do is put lipstick on them.

So early in the project, we just comb them. Now combing them is more complicated than you might think. Just like with women's fashion, the style is constantly changing. Sometimes the fashion says to comb them straight up. Then the style says to comb them straight forward. Next you have to comb them straight down. Then the fashion was straight down followed by straight forward. Dad tells of a time that you had a special comb that you'd pull across their bodies to make lines in their hair and then comb them straight up. It would make a pretty red steer look plaid.

So the fashion of my era is to comb them straight up. So I climb into the steer pen armed only with a curry comb and a spray bottle of Freibring's Winning Edge Conditioning Spray. I'm not sure exactly what it does, but it's pink and smells like strawberries. When applied to a steer, it smells like something pooped in a strawberry patch. But the spray is the most important part in giving "your steer a winning look."

My dad buys all of this stuff, but even he is a skeptic. "Somebody could pee in a bottle, give it a funny name, and sell it to some fool for $20 a bottle," he complains.

I stand as far away from my steer as I can and spray the pink mist onto him. My steer is a skeptic too…he is pretty sure that this little predator child is adding a marinade or some type of flavoring to his next meal. So I spray the conditioning spray and then start combing my steer up.

"Straight up," my Dad tells me.

"Okay," I respond, not sure how straight up is different from the direction I'm combing. T-bone is getting used to me, so he doesn't freak out any more, but he keeps a wary eye on me.

My Mom waltzes down to the steer barn to make a brief appearance.

"How's it going?" my Mom says as she surveys the battlefield.

"Pretty good," my Dad replies, "Nobody's been kicked or stepped on…yet."

Despite his perfect comedic timing, no one laughs.

"I just don't get it," my Mom says.

"What's that?" my Dad asks.

"Max is out here combing and primping his steer," my Mom says. I perk my attention in her direction. I sense a punchline coming aimed directly at me.

She continues, "All this fussing over his steers hair, and yet, he hasn't combed his own hair since last Sunday."

Everyone laughs. I pet my own head a couple of times with my hand to tame my wild hair, but the joke is on me.

"It's dinner time," my Mom says as she spins around and walks back up to the house.

My Mom operates a lot like the pony express. She's always on the move, staying busy keeping the house in order. But every now and then, just like the pony express, she stops in and leaves a message. Sometimes angry correction, but most of the time just a funny joke that makes everyone laugh.

"Let's turn 'em loose," my Dad says as he walks to T-bone and unties the lead rope from the post. He tosses the lead rope over the back of T-bones neck, a signal that T-bone did well. It will give him a brief respite from stepping on the lead rope. Stepping on their lead rope is also a training technique to help soften up their head. At least that's what Dad claims, though I think he just doesn't want to go through the effort of taking off and putting back on six lead ropes every day.

With their lead ropes out of the way, the steers buck and kick like range steers again. Then hunger takes over and they walk back to the feed trough to eat more. Every day, T-bone acts less and less like a range steer and more and more like a show steer.

Chapter Four
Ruined

Ruined is a word that my mother throws around rather casually. If I'm eating a burrito, without fail, the grease and burrito juice will drip out of the bottom of my burrito onto my shirt. My mother will shriek and look in horror at the blemish.

"That's a grease stain," my Mother bemoans. "Grease stains don't come out," she proclaims, indignantly. "Your shirt is ruined!"

And there it is, "ruined." It makes me want to take my shirt off and burn it, because it's "ruined." I'll just spend the rest of the day shirtless.

My Mother makes it out that my shirt is made out of a stain-o-phillic material and she will have to take my despoiled shirt down to the river like a Guatemalan washer woman. She will dip it alternatively in lye, tallow, and water, slapping it against the river rocks to wash my shirt, laboring for hours. But despite her best efforts, the stain is set and the shirt is ruined.

Or perhaps I'm wearing a Chinese paper shirt and my mother has to carefully steam it in a Chinese laundry. The process takes days to extract the burrito grease stain from my paper shirt. Even with the ancient secrets of the Orient, the stain is set and the shirt is ruined.

But the reality is my shirt is cotton and polyester and stains rarely set. My Mom sprays a magical elixir, called "Spray and Wash" on the stain, shakes her head at her progeny's chronic sloppiness, and then throws it in the washing machine. She twists a dial, flips a switch and walks away.

This magical machine spins and whirs and clangs and one hour later it will spin and shake and a pleasant sounding bell will ding. My Mom will remove the shirt, inspect it, see that the stain is gone, and shake her head again at her child's sloppiness. And the previously "ruined" shirt is as good as new.

Oh, sure, every now and then an imperceptible residue will remain, but it can only be seen under magnification. Maybe that is the world my mother fears. A world where busy body mothers wear magnification glasses and purple lights to identify mothers who let their children wear "ruined" shirts.

With all this said, there is one exception. Stay away from oil-based paints. If you spill oil-based paint on your shirt, you will wear that badge of incompetence for the remainder of that piece of clothing's lifetime. Come up with a good answer to the question, "Whatcha' been paintin'?"

Because you will get asked that over and over. And be prepared to listen to your mother complain about your "ruined" shirt every time you get to the bottom of your drawer and have to wear your paint shirt.

In the spring of the year, our prime cattle working season coincides with our rainy season. The snow melts and the ground becomes saturated. The rain falls and our normally dry soils turn to mud. The steers walk through the mud and churn it up real good. The grass is green and makes the cattle poop green and runny. They poop on the mud and churn it all together as they walk through the confinement of the corral. This creates a sticky, stinky slop...and the steers fling it everywhere. It gets on the fence, it gets slung onto the windshield of Dad's pickup, and it get all over everyone within a 100-foot radius from ground zero.

And the slop is indiscriminant. Laney is exceptionally vain and insists on foofing her hair and putting on lipstick. As the slop swirls around me like a January blizzard, an especially sloppy bit of muck slimes all over my face. A little bit of the slop gets into my mouth. Without taking time to taste the concoction, I gag and spit and do everything I can to remove the offending organic material from my mouth. I look for a clean spot on my hand to scrape my tongue. But there is no clean place on my hand. I look for a clean place anywhere, but there is none.

I look around and everyone is looking at me. They aren't sure whether to laugh or not.

"Open your mouth wider next time, Max," my Dad says. "That way, you won't get as much crap on your face."

Laugh…laugh is what they choose. With that simple line, everyone laughs. It's funnier if it's the other guy with dirt, water, and feces in their mouth, but I chuckle anyway. I hurry over to the water hydrant and rinse my mouth.

"Good thing we're done," My Dad says, "let's head back to the house and face Mom's wrath."

With all of this slop and muck flying around, I get to hear the "ruined" lecture. After we get done working the steers, we all walk up to the house. Even my Dad hangs his head in shame, knowing that he will hear the same "ruined" speech.

Dad opens the door and tentatively walks in first. My mother is on the other side of the house. My Dad slides into the mud room like a cat burglar and starts stripping off poopy clothing. Dad is an expert at escaping Mom's anger, so while the rest of us lolly-gag into the mud room, Dad is stripped down to his long johns and heading into the sanctuary of his office. Dad sits at his desk and hastily picks up the phone for a phone call.

This is a genius maneuver at my house. Our phone service is little better than a string and two steel cans. So when Dad is on the phone, we must be silent as the grave. Mom abides by this rule also, so there will be no yelling.

As we struggle to pull out of our "ruined" clothes, my mother yells at us in a whisper.

"You guys are making a huge mess in the mud room," my Mom whispers emphatically.

That's why they call it a mud room, I think to myself. *It's not the spotless room, or even the clean room.* I laugh on the inside. I'm not sure my Mom would see the humor in my comments.

My Mom holds my slop covered shirt up to the light. "That manure stain is set," she whispers as she glares at me, "that won't come out. Your shirt is ruined."

That's why I didn't wear my favorite shirt, I think to myself. *That's why I wore my white shirt that was washed with Laney's red socks and looks a little bit pink.* In my mind, it was already ruined.

"What do you have to say for yourself?" my Mother whispers.

"I should have ducked," I reply in answer, but it sounds more like a question.

"I can't believe you guys," my Mom whispers.

My Dad is still in the office. Dad isn't much of a talker, so he must have a long list of calls to make. He is locked safely away while the lecture from Mom continues.

"Do you know who has to do your laundry?" my Mom whispers.   "This mess is going to destroy my washing machine."

Mom is actually right on that account. The dirt, manure, and other organic material is just sticky enough to plug up a screen on the drain. It will plug up, Mom will play the damsel-in-distress, and my Dad will ride in to "fix" the "ruined" washing machine. He unhooks a hose, cleans out the junk, and reattaches the hose. He will usually go into a big production about how he has to gather all of his tools, consult the operator's manual and tap into all of his experience as a handy man. One set of pliers and three twists later, the washing machine will work again. My Mom will praise my Dad and talk about how he is her hero. But it was his pants and shirts that plugged it up in the first place. Mom does the same thing when the light stops working. She enlists Dad's skill as an electrician to "fix" the light. He climbs up a ladder, unscrews the light bulb, screws in another light bulb, and brings illumination back to the room with a flip of a switch. My Dad…a master electrician and plumber.

So Dad lingers in the office and Mom is alone now in the mud room, still whispering about all of the ruined clothing. Sometimes I think my Mom is a little bit crazy…and if she is, I'm pretty sure us kids made her that way.

When I'm at school, reading a book, I frequently come across a word that I'm not familiar with… "rotund" for instance.   I'll raise my hand to ask my teacher for a clarification and every time, she says those 6 evil words, "look it up in the dictionary." So I trudge back to the library to a giant collegiate dictionary that is open on an elevated lectern.

I flip through the pages singing silently to myself, "L-M-N-O-P...Q,R." There's the R's, then O and on through the pages until I find rotund.

rotund, adj. 1. Rounded in figure; plump.

This seems like the most useless skill imaginable. It would be great is someone could devise a machine where you could type in a word, or even better, just speak the word and that machine would spit out a definition of that word. If someone ever comes up with a device like that, I'll certainly buy one. And I'm not the only one. Whoever comes up with that will make hundreds...no thousands of dollars. It will probably be in the year 2010 when they have robots and flying cars and I can hardly wait.

But in the meantime, I will use my dictionary for evil. So the way my Mom used the word "ruined" seems overly dramatic to me, but I'm not sure. So I'll look it up in the dictionary. I have a paperback Roget's Collegiate Dictionary that the VFW Auxiliary gives out to all the school children in the area. I pull mine out and start flipping through the pages.

"L-M-N-O-P...Q,R," I sing slowly and out of rhythm. So there it is... "Ruined."

ruined, v. 1. The downfall, decay, or complete destruction of anything.

I want to emphasize the point of complete destruction. A little imperceptible blemish on a shirt doesn't describe completely destroyed. If I were to take my shirt out to the lawn, and lay it in front of the lawn mower. Dad would drive over it and it would be chopped into a million little pieces. That would be ruined.

Or if I sneaked a box of matches out of the kitchen…sneaked because Mom doesn't trust me with matches…out to the driveway. I would strike a match and touch the dancing flame to my shirt. The flame would spin tentatively around the hem until it catches and climbs to the collar. I drop the shirt to the dirt as it singes my fingers. The ball of shirt is completely consumed. All that remains is some smoldering ash. My shirt is "ruined." And my Mom is right…I shouldn't have matches.

This is a very slow time in working with show steers. All of us kids are busy with school. Mom is busy spring cleaning, which I don't understand. With mud covering every inch of our property, it is inevitable that we will track mud into the house. If it were me, I'd wait until June when the mud's all gone. But what am I talking about…it's not me.

Dad is really busy this time of year getting his steers and heifers ready to turn out on grass and getting the cows settled before they start having their calves.

So we wake up early in the morning and slog out to the steer pen. The sun hasn't quite peaked over the eastern mountains and the sky is a pallet of orange and regal purple. We pour out their grain and measure out some hay. Jerry checks their water trough because Dad will yell at Jerry if their water trough stops working.

We traipse through the mud back into the house. Mom has breakfast ready and has a sense of urgency that we will be late for school…and we will be.

I get to the mud room and pile all of my work coat, gloves, and boots in a neatly organized pile. I wash my hands, because if I don't, Mom will yell at me for being a slob…which I am by heredity and by nature. I hurry into the dining room and dig into the bowl of Cheerios that my Mom has made for me. I measure out two spoons full of sugar on the top and smother it all with milk.

One bite in, I hear my Mom yell, "Max!" I sit a little bit straighter in my chair and hastily swallow my partially chewed Cheerios. "I can smell you from here. Go wash your stinky hands."

I already washed my hands, I indignantly think to myself. I made the mistake of verbalizing that thought once. The lecture was long and painful. I learned my lesson so I dutifully walk back to the bathroom and wash my hands. I scrub and scrub and run my hands under lukewarm water, but they still stink a little bit. I don't know if Mom has a special technique or what, but I can never get my hands up to Mom standards. They look clean to me.

I scurry back to the table and finish my Cheerios. I leave the last three Cheerios floating in the milk. If I leave three Mom will be quietly annoyed. If I leave four, she'll yell at me for making a mess.

I run to the mudroom and throw on my boots and coat. I swing one strap of my backpack onto my right shoulder. I get to within two steps of the door when my Mom stops me.

"Max," she yells, "How many times do I have to tell you? Wash your hands before you head to school.

But I already did, I think to myself.

Again, I silently sulk to the bathroom and scrub my hands. I let the soap sit on my hands for a ten count and then place my hands under lukewarm water until my Mom yells that it's time to go. I shut off the water and dry them thoroughly. I sniff my hands and they smell like steer pen. I guess my hands are "ruined". I shove my "ruined" hands into my coat pocket to mask the smell and head off to school.

T-bone is getting fat. It seems like he is eating all the time. T-bone looks kind of funny because of all the mud. The mud, poop, slop mixture sticks to his hair and this slop hardens overnight. As T-bone walks, all of the dried mud bumps together and the clumps of mud get smooth and round. I think he looks like a tree full of fruit…and the jingling clumps are referred to as dingleberries.

Dad says when we weigh T-bone in, that we shouldn't get too excited because he has twenty-five pounds of dingleberries that we'll eventually wash off. But for now, T-bone proudly sports a full coat of dingleberries. *I wonder if T-bone's mother would chastise him about all of the dingleberries on his coat.*

I'm sure T-bone's cow would roll her big glassy cow eyes and say, "Mooooooo," which, of course, can be loosely translated as "it's ruined."

Chapter Five
Errors, the Disabled List, and All Things Baseball

I have a Grundig radio. It is my most treasured possession. If I switch it to shortwave, I can pick up radio signals from England, Holland, India, China, and Japan. But since I don't speak Chinese or Japanese, that feature is pretty useless. But I can pick up an AM signal from all over the country. I can listen to 850 out of Denver, or 770 out of Nebraska. I can even pick up AM stations from Canada and Mexico. But on a clear spring night, if all the conditions are just right, I can pick up eight or nine innings of a baseball game from San Francisco.

Now, I'm not a baseball player. There are eleven kids in my school and if someone can convince all eleven of us to play, we can field a batter, an umpire and nine players in the field. We rotate through every position. We can't really keep

score or play anything resembling a game, but we take turns pitching, batting, and playing the field. No, I'm not a player, but I do like to listen to baseball on the radio.

As the announcer describes the action, I listen intently to the statistics and all the numbers coming across the airwaves. I love how baseball people measure everything, whether it's important or not, and I love how bluntly specific they are about their statistics.

Most everyone really enjoys keeping track of hits, runs, RBIs, homeruns, and steals. Others like pitching statistics like strikeouts and ERA. But my favorite score keeping metric is the error.

On the official scoreboard at the baseball stadium, there are three important columns. Hits on the left, runs in the middle and errors on the right. The only column that really matters is runs. If you have the most runs, then you win the game.

But the error, now that is brutal in baseball. Imagine yourself as a second baseman for the New York Mets. Every night you have 40,000 fans cheering every play you make and booing every time you mess up. Those mess ups are killer. If you have a slow ground ball hit right to you, you field it cleanly and throw it hastily to the first baseman. If you throw the ball a matter of centimeters out of the reach of the first baseman, it will hurtle past him and into the bleacher. Forty thousand people will stand and boo your nascent throw. Millions of people listening on their radio or watching on TV will throw their hands in the air and yell at their broadcast device. And if that isn't enough, the official score keeper will place an E4 on his score card and the error will be recorded on the official scoreboard for the duration of the game. The poor second baseman will hit, catch and throw the rest of the game with that error lording over his shoulder. A monument of your futility, a scarlet letter of incompetence reminding all of the angry fans of your mistake. I'm glad there isn't an official scorekeeper tracking all of my mistakes.

The other baseball term that is brutal in its honesty is the disabled list. One of the features of baseball is that the teams are made up of only 25 players. Once the roster is set, there is a long series of rules that spell out how you can change players on the roster and the net result is it is difficult to change players.

This system works great except for when a player is injured. To account for injured players, a team can place said injured player on the disabled list and easily replace that player for anywhere from five days to thirty days depending on the injury.

Most of the time, it's a baseball injury. A blister on your pitching hand can get you on the five-day disabled list.

Twist your ankle sliding into home and you're on the ten-day disabled list.

Sometimes the disabled list is for other injuries. My Mom is a big fan of the Kansas City Royals. Her favorite player is George Brett and he once spent ten days on the disabled list because he had hemorrhoid surgery. Before that, I'd never heard of hemorrhoid surgery. It turns out that it's butt surgery. So, the poor guy not only has to have butt surgery, which sounds painful, but he also has to take ten days off and all of the sports pages in all of the newspapers in the country have to report why he's out…for butt surgery.

I enjoy listening to baseball, but I don't ever want to play the game. I hate making mistakes and I hate being hurt. What would make it even worse is that the scorekeeper is going to keep track of my mistakes and all of my hurts and injuries will be broadcast to the world. And when I'm working with steers, there are a lot of mistakes and injuries to report.

I'm pretty new at working with steers. It's my Dad's occupation and he's been working with steers since he took a 4-H steer to the fair when he was a kid. He really knows what he's doing…and I really have no idea what I'm doing. Sudden movements will make your steer freak out. They'll pull against their halter until you're sure they will pull the fence over. But if I move too slow, I'll get yelled at to hurry up or get out of the way.

One of the biggest mistakes that you can make is when you're feeding and watering your steer. Most people think that feed is the most important thing in feeding a steer. They are partially right. But the most critical nutrient that steers need is water. Without water, a steer will stop gaining after a few hours and will die of thirst after a few days. So the water needs to be checked every day.

But because water is so important, my oldest brother Jerry is responsible for the water. If my steer goes without water for an afternoon, then Jerry gets yelled at. I wish all of the mess up and errors resulted in Jerry getting yelled at instead of me.

During the course of a spring and summer, there are innumerable opportunities for errors. I counted and there are one-million, four hundred seventy-three thousand, eight hundred thirty-one chances to mess up during the course of my project. I got an error for exactly half. And of those, I got yelled at for twenty-five thousand, eight hundred ninety-nine of them. To be completely honest, I didn't really count, but I know I get yelled at a lot for my errors.

"Max, you fed too much!" "Max, you didn't feed enough!" "Max, don't pet him on the head!" "Max, don't spill the hair spray!" "Max, you stink!" That last one was Laney. She doesn't need much of an excuse to yell at me.

It's barely June and the errors are really starting to add up. Dad is very reassuring. He'll tell me that mistakes are how we learn. If that's the case, then I am learning a whole lot as my project progresses.

A rarity in baseball is an error that leads to the disabled list. I actually asked my Dad if he could remember an error that led to an injury that put a player on the disabled list. He couldn't remember it happening, but he said it has most likely happened…probably…maybe. But in training steers, an error can lead directly to the disabled list.

It is reasonable to question the parenting skills of a father who hands their 12-year-old little boy a thousand-pound steer. The steer wears a thin rope halter that applies slight pressure to the nose…with an emphasis on the word slight. The parent hands this thin rope to their little boy with the only direction, "Hold on tight…Don't let go." It may not be enough to question the parenting skills of that father. It may be more appropriate to question the sanity of that parent.

That is the situation I find myself, Max Hackberry, in. We are past tying T-bone to a post. He walks easily behind the Massey-Ferguson tractor. My Dad has pulled him around the pen a couple of times. He says it's time for T-bone to learn how to work for me.

"Hold on tight, Max," my Dad tells me, "Hold his head up high…you'll have more control."

I lift on his head, but T-bone doesn't want to lift his head, so it doesn't go up. That's a nice summary of how my interaction leading T-bone goes. We basically do exactly what T-bone wants to. I want to obey my father's command of keeping T-bone's head up. T-bone, on the other hand, wants to drop his head to the ground to eat grass. So, despite my strenuous effort, T-bone drops his head and eats.

I want to walk T-bone and me forward. T-bone wants to stand. So we stand. If I want to stop, and T-bone wants to keep walking, we keep walking. You get the picture here.

I grip the lead rope tightly and pull forward. After a dozen futile try's, T-bone takes a step and off we go. T-bone takes precisely seven steps at a pleasant pace, and T-bone suddenly wants to walk faster. So we walk faster.

And then suddenly, T-bone jumps and bucks and kicks. I hold on as best as I can, but the rope slips out of my hand and T-bone bucks across the pen.

Now when I say buck, I don't want to give the wrong impression. When you go to a rodeo and watch the bull riding, the bulls jump and kick. The bulls will jump in a tight circle and the bull kicks its legs high above its head. That's not how T-bone bucks.

We can draw an analogy from basketball. Magic Johnson is a basketball player. He is six feet nine inches tall and very athletic. He dribbles as graceful as a swan. He passes the ball easily and his shot could be in a textbook as how to shoot a basketball. When he drives to the basket, he soars through the air and dunks the ball.

Every year, the county police and the county fire department have a charity basketball game. It's a bunch of middle-aged guys playing a basketball game. They are out of shape. The firemen have an advantage because they have access to oxygen tanks. Most of the guys wear head bands on their heads. Dad can empathize…he's bald too and says a head band is the only way to keep sweat out of their eyes. All of the players at the charity basketball game pass, dribble, and shoot…just like Magic Johnson. Both games are called basketball, but one is comprised of professional athletes and the other is still looking for their first athlete.

Now that is probably a longer than necessary analogy to make my point, but the analogy is sound. Rodeo bulls could be considered professional athletes…just like Magic Johnson. In contrast to that, my slightly overweight, thoroughly unathletic steer is more like the charity basketball players. He tries real hard to buck and kick, but it just looks awkward and clumsy.

So we return to our story with T-bone bucking and lumbering across the steer pen. He enjoys his freedom, running across the pen unencumbered by the predator child and his rope. But in his excitement, he steps in a rodent hole and wrenches his ankle. With the sudden pain, he stops bucking and limps over to the corner of the pen.

"You can't let go," my Dad exclaims. It sounds a lot like yelling, but he will rarely admit to yelling.

"I tried, but he got away,"

"You have to go across the nose to get him to stop," my Dad explains. Thirty years from now I can picture myself, in similar exasperation as my father, will tell my child, "Go across the nose to get him to stop," and even at that point, not really knowing what it means or how it stops a steer.

"He's turned up lame, Max," my Dad says as he grabs T-bone's lead rope.

"Lame?" I ask. "How's that?"

"When you let go of him, he stepped in that hole and hurt his foot."

So, that is obviously an error on my part. I see that imaginary scorekeeper placing a 1 under the E in the last column next to my name. I'm used to errors at this point, but the injury is something new.

"So what does that mean?" I ask. "Can I still take him to the fair?"

"I don't know."

I don't know. My Dad always has an answer. It's not always the right answer, but always an answer. This *I don't know* is something new and different.

"So what do we do?" I ask.

"Go get the water hose hooked up. We'll run cold water over it for a few minutes to keep it from swelling. I'll go call Doc Asdale and see if there's anything we can give him.

My Dad ties up T-bone and heads to the house. I get the hose ready and spray cold water onto T-bone's foot. It looks just fine to me, but he limps with every step. I get bored, so I start spinning the stream of water in circles and figure eights, but always keeping the water on the T-bone's leg.

After about 10 minutes, my Dad comes back with one of my Mom's freshly baked chocolate chip cookies in his mouth and two in his hand. I used to think those extras were to share with his children. But my father's love for my Mom's cookies rival only his love for my mother herself. I genuinely believe my Mom's cookies is why my Dad married my Mom. That's really the only reason that makes sense to me.

"Doc Asdale says we can give him a shot of LA-200," my Dad says. "The withdrawal is 45 days and we're almost 85 days out."

"What's a withdrawal?" I ask.

"It's the number of days before slaughter that you can't give a medicine anymore."

I wince at the word slaughter. My Dad has the syringe and needle full of the medicine and ready for the shot. He quickly throws one cookie in each cheek. He sticks the needle into T-bone and depresses the plunger. T-bone hardly notices until Dad pulls the needle out. T-bone throws his head and strains against his halter.

"I wouldn't get too close for the next couple of days," my Dad says. "He's going to be a little edgy."

I listen to my Dad's words as I pull the hose back around T-bone. I think I'm out of reach of T-bone, but he kicks and his club like foot smashes my knee. I groan and drop to the ground.

"Max, are you okay?" my Dad asks as he pulls me away from T-bone, so I don't get kicked again.

"It hurts," I groan. Tears sting my eyes, but it hurts too much to cry.

"Let me help you," my Dad says. "We need to get you up and get some ice on your knee."

The treatment sounds very familiar. My Dad is giving me the same treatment that we gave T-bone.

"Are you going to give me shot of LA-200?" I ask my Dad.

He chuckles. "I'll give you some Bayer aspirin. We'll save the LA-200 for the steers."

My Dad settles me onto the couch and places a bag of peas on my knee. Nobody eats peas in my family, but we have one bag in the freezer that we always use for such occasions.

"I told you not to get too close for the next couple of days," my Dad says matter-of-factly.

"*I told you so*" is the last thing I want to hear. Do parents really think that an I-told-you-so is really the best thing in this situation. They don't say it for the benefit of their child. I guess they are just trying to clear their conscience.

As I sit on the couch, and wait for the effects of the aspirin to kick in, I quickly go over the score in my mind. This is my second error today. The first error put T-bone on the disabled list. And the second one put me on the disabled list. I should tell everyone to stay away from me...I'm just a medical disaster waiting to happen.

I was worried about the injuries. And I was worried because my Dad was worried. But the LA-200 worked because T-bone stopped limping after about five days. So I will probably spend the next twenty years administering LA-200 to my animals for every injury or sickness that they have...whether it does anything or not.

And as for me, the pain in my knee went away after a couple of days. It didn't even bruise, which is annoying because a bruise is the best way to show the world that you're injured. Of sure, a cast conveys an injury very well, but you have to break something to earn a cast. No, the bruise is perfect, and I couldn't even get a bruise for my effort.

When the final score was tallied, I had two errors and a five-day stint on the disabled list. T-bone had one hit...his hoof to my knee. T-bone learned a valuable lesson...Don't let your enthusiasm get the best of you. And I learned a valuable lesson...never trust a show steer. As June turns to July, T-bone keeps getting fatter, and I learn these important, but sometimes painful lessons.

Chapter Six
Girls,
and Other Useless Things

When I think of useless things, 4-H camp is the first thing that pops into my head. Summer camp is full of useless things.   Campfire songs are cheesy and lack important elements like beat, rhythm, and tune. I prefer a good country music song to any campfire song.

And all the silly games at summer camp…I just don't get them. Most of the games are pointless, lacking skill and objective and others are so far beyond pointless to be gross. The silly games are just useless.

All of the outdoorsy stuff is pretty useless too. We live up in the hills where I sleep in a nice comfortable bed with modern conveniences like electricity and indoor plumbing. But to go to summer camp we have to ride for three hours in a school bus to a camp ground in someone else's hills to sleep in a sleeping bag on a bunk with limited electricity and one bathroom in the middle of the campground. I just don't get the appeal.

But the worst is the dance. 4-H camp is a co-ed program. Co-ed just means that we have to put up with girls. And because it's a co-ed program, we go to a co-ed camp. Because there are both boys and girls at the camp, the camp organizers think it's a great idea to have a dance. Even if I enjoyed dancing, or was good at dancing, it really is a useless pursuit…I mean really, what's the point of dancing?

But I go to 4-H camp and you may be wondering why. 4-H camp is the best chance I have to see my friends during the summer. There are some serious geographical distances between me and my friends during the summer. I get to see some of my friends at school and others at church. Some, friends I only see at 4-H activities. My best friend is my cousin, Benny. I go to school with him, I go to church with him, and we get to see each other a lot. But not enough in the summer time. We live about fifteen miles apart and that is considerably farther than I want to ride my bike. So the only time I get to see Benny is at 4-H activities. And the longest 4-H activity outside of the fair is 4-H camp. So despite all of the short comings, we both go to 4-H camp.

The ride to 4-H camp is very exciting…for about the first two minutes. We don't ride school buses to school…there aren't enough kids to justify a bus so all of the parents drive their kids to school.

So Mom puts me on a school bus at the 4-H office in Twin Falls. The school bus is novel and we all chirp like a hungry flock of chicks. But once we cross the canyon, the novelty wears off and we are stuck on a hot bus on a winding road. Mercifully, we stop just north of Shoshone. There is a fancy new rest area in the middle of nowhere and everyone uses the facilities. All of the adults scare us into trying because this is the "last bathroom that doesn't look like a sagebrush at the side of the road."

We drive for another forty-five minutes where we make an unscheduled stop. As we start winding through the canyons and along creeks, there is always one camper who gets car sick. If we're lucky, they get the bus stopped and he pukes at the side of the road. If we're not lucky, he will toss his cookies in the aisle and we have to suffer through the stench for the next forty-five minutes until we're there.

I'm not exactly sure what it is, but there is a lot of throwing up and crying the first day of 4-H camp. We haven't even made it to Sawtooth 4-H camp and we've had our first barfer. There is typically a couple more at lunch, a handful of upchucks when the snack bar opens, and then a few more at dinner. Without fail, one camper will throw up overnight. And if you ate the slop they feed us, you'd understand all the vomit.

But the crying…I don't get that at all. Most of the kids crying are missing their parents. That's not me at all. Getting away from my parents for a couple of days is as good for me as it is for them. Distance makes the heart grow fonder…or distance is what keeps mammals from eating their young.

The first day is really about getting oriented to camp life. We have to play a bunch of get-to- know-you games. It would make more sense to just have a mixer and we could mingle with each other, shaking hands and introducing ourselves to each other. That would be far too sophisticated and to be perfectly honest, it just wouldn't happen.

So instead, we sing the Banana Name Song. The song is so simple that it could be considered stupid. You just take a person's name and add different letters to their name and say, "banana."

For instance, "Max, Max, bo bax, banana fana, fo fax, me mi mo Max, Maaax." Everyone sings it and I have gone from an anonymous camper to a name that everyone knows, but nobody remembers.

Benny is next, "Benny Benny, bo benny, banana fana, fo fenny, me mi mo menny, Benny." That's how the Benny song should go, except Benny figured out that there are four names that can be inserted into the Banana Name Song that causes everyone at 4-H camp to enthusiastically yell out a bad word. And Benny claimed his name was one of those four names. It amazes me how fast the camp director can show up from out of nowhere and shut down an activity when an obscenity is yelled at camp…even when it is inadvertent. Regardless, Benny is a hero amongst our circle of friends because silly songs and get-to-know-you games are finished for the day.

With the setting of the sun, all of the weary campers head to their cabins for the night. Cabins are assigned and the assignment is critical to a fun 4-H camp. I've heard that at other camps, the campers get assigned cabins at random and then each cabin is given a name. Usually, the cabins are given Indian names, or more commonly an anglicized faux Indian name like the Wahoo Cabin or the Wheretheheckarewe Cabin.

But at 4-H camp we are segregated by species…or to be more accurate, by the species of our project. All of us beef kids are in one cabin. All of the sheep kids are in a cabin, the swine kids have a cabin and the horse kids have a cabin. And then there is a mixed cabin for home arts and all of the small species like goats, rabbits and poultry.

Instead of a fancy Indian name, each cabin is assigned a color. I know it's not very creative, but it is probably more culturally sensitive than other camps. With this system, we are in the blue cabin.

So the pranks are notorious at 4-H camp…and they begin the first night. The first one is pretty simple. Benny had the foresight to bring the shaving cream and a feather. Benny decided Willie Nichols would be perfect for this one. As quietly as possible, Benny sprays shaving cream on Willie's hand and with the feather, he tickles Willie's nose. Without waking, Willie subconsciously pulls his hand up to his nose to scratch the itch. When he does, the shaving cream smears all over his face.

Willie wakes up to shaving cream smeared all over his face, perpetrated by his own hand. We all laugh and carry on at poor Willie's misfortune.

Then there is the overnight prank that by far gives you the most bang for your buck. It's called "Truck" and is by far the most complicated one to pull off. To get the truck to work, you really need at least four people, but six is better. Each individual action is fairly simple, but everything must be orchestrated and timed perfectly. You need a pillow man, two flash lighters and then the cautionary yellers.

A victim is chosen. Benny brought the flashlight, so Benny chooses Eric Woodson to abruptly awaken. The pillow man slaps Eric to awaken him. Simultaneously, the two flash lighters standing above Eric turn their flashlights on and everyone involved yells, "Truck." The poor chap interrupts his sweet dreams to see two lights coming at him with everyone yelling, "truck." Despite falling asleep comfortably in his bunk dozens of miles from the nearest highway, his brain quickly analyzes all of the stimuli and determines that he has floated to the nearest highway and has awaken to a crowd of

other boys yelling "truck" with an actual truck barreling down on him.

Screams are normal and sometimes even tears. All of the perpetrators laugh uncontrollably. Poor Eric is still shaking as the laughter subsides. We all give Eric high fives and he assures us that he gets the joke and there's no hard feelings…but Eric will never sleep soundly again.

4-H camp always wakes to the sounds of a trumpet. I think they call the wake-up song Reveille…but the song that is played sounds more like the call to post at a horse race crossed with a goose that has been caught by a coyote. Lights out is every night at 9:30 and the wake up is at 6:30. If everyone went to sleep at 9:30, nine hours is plenty of sleep for kids our age. But nobody actually went to sleep at 9:30.

Breakfast is unidentifiable, and then it is straight into arts and crafts. Benny likes to call it "farts and crap," and that's probably more accurate. Something is salvaged from the garbage, it is glued together and painted and then we have something to take home to our parents as proof that we did something at 4-H camp.

Lunch is a blander version of breakfast and I think our stomachs are getting used to the slop because no one throws up at lunch. We have a little time back at our cabins and then the afternoon is devoted to games and competitions between the cabins. Throughout the camp, there is no pavement, no concrete, no nothing…except for the basketball/volleyball court, which is paved with asphalt. The only paving material that would be more dangerous to play a sporting event would be a court paved with shards of glass. So we play volleyball where no one makes too great of an effort to avoid a fall and a certain flesh wound. After that we play the most polite basketball game imaginable. Even the biggest bully won't push you down because a fall could result in attempted murder charges.

In addition to the actual sporting games, there are also some more silly competitions. For instance, a Twinkie eating contest, or an egg on the spoon race. These are all neat and fun, but I was a witness to the most epic contest in the history of 4-H camp. It is a classic Chubby Bunny contest that turned into a World Record performance.

Five boys were chosen, one for each cabin. Four of the boys were anonymous and will fade into the abyss of history. But the representative from our cabin is Randy Wainwright. Little do we know that we are on the verge of witnessing history.

Now the rules of Chubby Bunny are fairly simple. Each competitor places a marshmallow in their mouth and without swallowing, must say, "Chubby Bunny," without losing the marshmallow. As we see with the first few marshmallows, this task is no problem. But the more marshmallows the harder it gets. And the winner of the competition is the camper that can fit the most marshmallows in their mouth and still say, "Chubby Bunny."

The competition falls off quickly. The first camper breaks and spits up his marshmallows after five. The second and third give up simultaneously at twelve marshmallows. So the competition comes down to our representative, Randy Wainwright, and the camper from the swine cabin named Mickey Barlow. At fifteen marshmallows, poor Mickey turns green, but Randy Wainwright blurts out, "Chubby Bunny," without a single foamy, white drool.

Now Randy Wainwright and Mickey Barlow are big kids…which isn't saying much because most everyone is big compared to me. But being big isn't enough to win a Chubby Bunny contest. You have to have a wide, square jaw. Naturally, it helps to have big cheeks. And the most critical quality to winning a Chubby Bunny contest is a very inactive gag reflex.

I would be a terrible Chubby Bunny competitor because I have a very active gag reflex. I usually barf when I go to the dentist. If I see someone vomit, I will start making cat-trying-to-dislodge-a-hairball noises. So throughout the contest, I have trouble watching and spend most of the time dry heaving. But I know I'm witnessing something special so I can't look away.

They reach twenty marshmallows and it is obvious who is going to win. Mickey Barlow has gone cross-eyed and Randy Wainwright looks like he is enjoying tea at his grandmother's house.

Twenty-one is it. Mickey gets the "Chubby" out, but halfway through "Bunny," all of the marshmallows spill onto the ground. Mickey will be sick for the rest of 4-H camp.

But Randy Wainwright is just getting started. No one is sure what drove him on, he was obviously the winner. Twenty-three Chubby Bunnies, twenty-four Chubby Bunnies, twenty-five Chubby Bunnies. With no one else, the marshmallows come faster now. The crowd is cheering wildly and chanting the number in unison.

At twenty-eight marshmallows, one of the camp counsellors looks up from a rule book that he's been consulting and says, "The world record is thirty-three."

Thirty-three I think to myself, *he could do this*.

At thirty marshmallows, Randy hesitates, but still utters the indubitable phrase, "Chubby Bunny."

The crowd has stopped counting and now chants, "Chubby Bunny…Chubby Bunny," over and over again. Thirty-one Chubby Bunnies…Thirty-two Chubby Bunnies…Thirty-three Chubby Bunnies. Randy Wainwright stands at the edge of greatness. His massive cheeks are so full they could pop. He can't possibly fit another marshmallow in his mouth.

Randy purses his lips slightly and stuffs the marshmallow in his face. The crowd falls silent, listening for the two fateful words. Time seems to slow down as Randy confidently says, "Chubby Bunny." He's done it. World Record holder Randy Wainwright. Randy was able to fit two more marshmallows into his mouth, but that was the end. I am convinced he could have fit more, but the counselors ran out of marshmallows.

And poor Randy isn't sure what to think. Since that epic afternoon, Randy has had the nickname of Chubby Bunny…a rather inglorious nickname for someone of his achievement.

The last day of 4-H camp is designed to get all of the campers tired so they will sleep on the bus ride home instead of causing trouble. There is the same early morning wake up followed by a five-mile hike to Alturus Lake. After that is more games, and then after dinner is a campfire where we sing campfire songs and then following the campfire is the dance.

The counselors don't have any time between the campfire and the dance, so we have to be ready for both. We all have to take a shower at the insistence of our counselors. They have a community shower with no privacy so the real challenge becomes how to take a shower without taking your clothes off. We dress up in our best clothes and we all shine our cowboy boots because Johnny Morton brought a shoe shine kit. Everyone then slathers on some Old Spice cologne that Tyler Sampson "borrowed" from his dad.

Then we head to the campfire. It turns out that Old Spice is actually an attractant for mosquitos, so I get swarmed by the little blood suckers and will end up itching the bites for the next week. The smoke from the campfire swirls around and encircles all of the campers. So all of the effort to smell fresh and clean has literally gone up in smoke.

Sufficiently skeeter bitten and thoroughly smoke riddled, we walk back to the Mess Hall. The tables have all been folded up and the benches line the outside wall. All of the girls sit on the South wall and all of the boys sit on the North wall. The lights are all turned out except for some Christmas light on the front table and the back of the room that reflect a disco ball hanging down from the ceiling.

The music is WAY too loud. All of the windows are open but it is still hot and stuffy. We all sweat like crazy…now we smell smoky and stinky.

Benny and Randy have positioned themselves on a bench under a handrail near the door. Both Benny and Randy have hooked their arms around the rail so that the girls can't drag them onto the dance floor. In reality, the hordes of girls at camp aren't clamoring to dance with anyone…much less Randy and Benny.

The next song comes on and the counselor playing the music pulls out his cheap microphone and in a garbled, tinny voice says, "The next song, everyone one has to dance. Anyone not dancing will be thrown in the lake."

Everyone scurries to find a dancing partner. The only thing worse than dancing with a girl would be swimming in a glacial lake. Benny and Randy stay at their post with arms hooked…now to avoid a late-night swim.

I apprehensively walk around the mess hall looking for someone to dance with. To me, it's easier to pick a steer than to pick a dancing partner. And with both, I really don't know what I'm looking for. Most of the other campers are more decisive than I am so my choices are rapidly narrowing.

I walk up to Melanie Sneldon and ask her to dance. "I don't dance with dorks," she says. I look around and there are three others boys without dancing partners and we are all dorks. *I hope you enjoy your swim,* I think to myself.

I walk a little further and to a shy girl named Amy Futterman. She stares at the floor, hoping to go unnoticed. I dash her hopes, walking over to her.

"Would you like to dance?" I ask, self-consciously. I'm not really sure how this ritual is supposed to go. I'm not sure if I'm supposed to extend my hand and bow…I'm not even sure if I'm asking the right question.

Amy looks up, blinks twice, and says with a half-smile, "Sure."

I was really hoping she would say no. Should I grab her hand? *The less touching the better,* I think to myself.

It's a fast song, mercifully, something by AC/DC I think. We face each other and shuffle awkwardly to the left and to the right. I'm pretty sure I'm doing it wrong. I'm not sure what to do with my hands.

"My name is Max," I mumble, not sure if conversation is appropriate.

"What," Amy yells back. The music is really loud.

"My name is Max," I yell.

"I know," Amy yells back. "My name is Amy."

"I know," I reply. With the music blaring, conversation is impractical even if it is appropriate.

The music fades out and everyone stops dancing. The counselor playing the cassette tapes gives direction on his microphone again. "Girls choice," he says.

Without sitting down, Amy asks, "Would you like to dance?"

"Sure," I reply, unaware that the next song is a slow song.

The problem with a slow song is that it involves all of the awkwardness of a fast dance, but is enhanced because touching is involved.

I was taught that for a dance to be appropriate, you should be at least a Bible distance away from your dancing partner. To be safe, I decide to maintain a space of the Roget's Collegiate Dictionary, my Dad's Animal Nutrition college textbook, and one copy of War and Peace distance away. I would have preferred to be farther away, but my arms aren't that long.

The slow Bryan Adams song blasts over the loud speakers. Everyone is sweating, but I wonder if I'm the only one that is self-conscious about it. We sway back and forth lacking rhythm and grace and generally resembling a pair of weeble-wobbles.

"So which cabin are you with?" I ask, trying to ease the tension with small talk.

"I'm in the horse cabin," she says. "We all take horses to the fair."

Obviously, I think to myself to avoid being rude. "I'm in the beef cabin," I reply.

"The beef cabin…huh," she says. "I don't think I could eat my project."

Because horse meat is gross, I think to myself. "I don't eat my project. We put him on the truck at the fair and I get a really big paycheck from the sale."

"The money would be nice," she says politely. Finally, something we can agree with.

The song ends and I step away from my dancing partner before the final echo bounces off the wall.

"I'll maybe see you at the fair," I say. I don't know why I say that. I could care less if I see her at the fair.

"I doubt it," Amy says. "You'll be at the steer barn and I'll be at the horse barn."

"Well…bye," I say, not knowing what else to say.

And just like that, the silence is over and 4-H camp is winding down. I'll go another month or so until I get to see Benny again, but it'll be good to get back and see T-bone.

At this point in my project, T-bone's gluttony is helping him put on some needed fat. It looks like T-bone has been playing a daily match of Chubby Bunny. But instead of marshmallows, he's been stuffing his cheeks with grain and hay. T-bone could easily be called Chubby Bunny.

Chapter Seven
$@#&-ing bad words

In 1939, the movie "Gone with the Wind" made cinematic history by saying the first bad word in the history of film. The very handsome Clark Gable looks deep into the eyes of Vivian Leigh playing Scarlet O'Hara and says, "Frankly my dear, I don't give a d@#$." And with that seemingly innocuous phrase, the movie ends and the movie business would never again be the same.

Forty-seven years later, it is hard to watch a movie where you don't hear at least a couple of bad words. It got so bad, in fact, that the Supreme Court of the United States of America has created a list of 7 words that can't be said on television. Those are known as the "big seven" and I know that if I use one of the big seven bad words, then my Mom will lose her mind.

You may think I am exaggerating just a little bit, but it's true. If I say one of the big seven swear words, my mother's sanity leaves her and she will try to poison me. Soap is a poison…right?

Anyway, she will wash my mouth out with soap. I guess she is using an analogy, the soap will clean my dirty mouth, but all of the warning labels on the soap clearly state, "for external use only," which implies poison in my mind.

I have actually become somewhat of a connoisseur. Ivory is by far the blandest, it has hardly any flavor at all. Zest is without question the worst tasting. I would describe it as a mix of fireplace ash and throw up. Irish Spring is without a doubt the best flavored soap. It tastes like a cucumber with just a hint of mint. I'm not sure that I want my next bowl of ice cream to taste like Irish Spring, but as far as soap goes, it is the best.

Dad has a more nuanced approach to cursing. For the most part, you'll never hear Dad swear. I've never seen Mom wash Dad's mouth out with soap, but I've never seen Dad swear around Mom. Evidently, she has him trained.

But Dad has a different tolerance for bad words based on the situation. For instance, Dad will give me a glare if I say "dang it" at church. I know better than to utter anything stronger. I can get away with a little bit more around my friends at school and I'm okay if I stay away from the previously mentioned big seven from the Supreme Court, but there is a place where a lot of bad words are tolerated. When we are at the barnyard or at the ranch, we can get away with what's referred to as "barnyard language."

When a carpenter is banging a hammer on a particularly stubborn nail, and that carpenter slams the hammer onto his thumb, he will yell out in pain, "$#*i*&." There are sometimes that a "shucks," or a "dang it" will work. But the shooting pain of a self-inflicted hammer hit can only be assuaged with one of the big seven.

And so it goes with barnyard language. If you get kicked in the shin by a steer, a "doggone it" won't quite cut it. I can get away with a full out swear word in this situation without tasting soap.

Or say you slam your hand in a closing gate. Pain shoots directly from your injured hand to that place in your brain that inhibits a steady flow of bad words. Your mouth reflexively opens and an expletive spills out. If it is a door at home, my Mom will tend to my injured hand, and then march me down to the bathroom to wash my mouth out with soap. But instead, the coarse word is at least overlooked and more likely, accepted. Because of the relaxed rules at the barnyard, ranch and steer pen, I spend as much time as I can at these locations. It's probably the only thing saving my taste buds from permanent damage from the soap.

Dad says it's a little like the song, "Home on the Range." Remember the line, "And *never* is heard, a discouraging word, and the skies are not cloudy all day." Remember that, or does it seem a little bit off. The line is, "And *seldom* is heard, a discouraging word, and the skies are not cloudy all day." Even the most optimistic cowboy song ever written accounts for the inevitable slip of the tongue.

One last thought on bad words. When I read the newspaper, I tend to focus on the comic strips. There is about a dozen strips in our newspaper and everybody has their favorite. Jerry likes "Hagar the Horrible." Jimmy always reads "The Wizard of Id" and Laney's favorite comic strip is "Garfield." That's a good one if you can handle a talking cat. In the world I live in, a talking cat would creep everybody out. Mom likes "The Family Circle." It is the only single pane comic strip so I guess that's all she has time for. And Dad just reads the rest of the paper…completely skipping over the comics.

My favorite comic strip is "Beetle Bailey." It's about a private in the army who is always messing up and getting yelled at by the Sarge. I'm not really into the army, but I can relate with Beatle Bailey. So the army is a lot like the barnyard…they use a lot of choice words and harsh language. But the newspaper can't print the big seven bad words and for community standards, they don't print any bad words. To show all of the curse words that Sarge hurls at Beatle, they use all of the symbols above the numbers on the type writer. From left to right, that is !,@,#,$,%,^,&,*,(,), and sometimes ?. For some reason, curse words are typically four-letter words. The comic strip uses four randomly chosen symbols to signify swearing. That's the way it's shown in this book too. The author has an expectation that his mother will read this book and doesn't want his mouth washed out with soap.

If you're reading this book aloud and you come across a #$&!, simply stick your tongue out and blow raspberries. This is the most reasonable way to say any unspeakable word.

August gets really busy with my steer project. Things that have been put off and procrastinated can no longer be put off. With less than a month before the fair, the list of things we still need to do is a lot longer than the time than the time we have to do it. Feeding is more critical than ever because our steers aren't quite fattened. And they still need more training on leading, setting up their feet, and standing. We have to keep then clean and we need to get all of their hair clipped.

But the biggest project left is hoof trimming. Now hoof trimming is not something a boy can do. It is, without a doubt, a man's job. It requires a significant amount of strength and endurance, and some specialized equipment.

My Dad owns a hoof trimmer. A hoof trimmer is a bright red chute that you lead your steer into. The head catch V's together but also has a bar that slides down to keep the steer in place. The squeeze isn't lever driven; it is a giant ratcheting winch. It's like someone took all of the elements of a properly functioning squeeze chute and altered it to make it almost unusable.

There are a couple of straps that go under the steers belly, and then the chute and the immobilized steer and chute tips over. With the steer on his side, my Dad can easily work on his hooves…well not easily, but at least he has access.

So I lead T-bone into the contraption and Dad pulls all the right levers and twists all of the knobs. Then he turns the winch and T-bone is tipped over. Dad pulls out an electrical grinder and starts grinding chunks of hoof off of T-bone. T-bone struggles. From his memory, nothing good happens when you're restrained and tipped on your side. Dad grinds until just before the hoof starts to bleed. If he grinds until just after it starts to bleed, Dad will say a bad word.

Dad flips the grinder switch to the off position and he flips the ratchet on the winch and tips the chute back to standing. Dad trips the lever to open the squeeze on the chute, but it doesn't open. He hits it a couple of times with his palm, but the lever doesn't open. He reaches around a post and smacks the lever again. The lever pops up and the squeeze springs open. Before my Dad can pull his arm out of the way, his arm gets slammed between the squeeze and the frame. My Dad's arm is crushed between the two chunks of steel like a stick caught between the two sides of a scissor.

"%$@&," my Dad yells out in pain. Now everyone knows that there is a hierarchy of curse words. Beyond the Supreme Courts big seven bad words are the worst of the worst. We can describe them as the royalty of curse words. But even among the royalty, some swear words are much worse than others…Not the jester or the Earl of Vulgarities, the word my Dad yelled was the King of the curse words.

Shocked by the discouraging word I just heard, I stand there in disbelief.

"Help, Max," My Dad yells in pain, "get this $%*#ing thing off of me."

It turns out that curse words aren't just nouns, they can be verbs, adverbs, adjectives and present participle verbs. Swear words are very versatile portions of language. As I ponder the niceties of grammar and syntax of bad words, I jump into action. I pull off the latch and the squeeze on the chute moves slightly. It's just enough for my Dad to pull his arm out of the bind.

"Are you okay?" I ask.

"I'm not sure," my Dad replies with his arm dangling motionless at his side. Usually when he gets a bump or bruise, he'll flex the injured arm, but this time it just hangs there.

"Is it broken?" I ask.

"I don't know, Max," my Dad replies, enunciating each word. I can tell he is exasperated and I better shut up and let him be.

"Can you get T-bone put away?" My Dad asks.

"I can," I reply confidently. My Dad looks at me to judge how confident I appear.

"Are you sure?" my Dad asks between gasps of pain.

"I'm sure I can," I reply, this time making a conscious effort to sound confident.

"I'm going to the house," my Dad says.

I hurry to slide T-bone out the back of the chute. As I lead T-bone back to his corral, my mind races…trying to process what just happened. Dad didn't' say anything about the bad word he uttered. He didn't say, "I'm sorry." He didn't say, "pardon my French." Which reminds me, when a Frenchman nearly breaks his arm and curses in French, does he tell his friends, "Pardonnez mon Anglais." Or is French really that foul mouthed of a language? Who really knows, but I wish Dad would have said something.

Should I tell Mom? Would Mom wash Dad's mouth out with soap? I always assumed that Dad said a swear word once or twice around Mom after they first got married and that Mom washed his mouth out with soap. I just assumed that Dad is a faster learner than us kids and never cursed again. If that isn't the case, I would most certainly chalk this up as a double standard that us kids are constantly suffering from.

Perhaps this is one of the exceptions to swearing. We are close enough to the barn that this could be considered a barnyard language zone. Or perhaps this is just one of those "seldom" time that a discouraging word is heard on our home range.

I know that there are even swear words that you can say at church. But they are not really swear words. But they sound a lot like swear words. It's a homonym…two words that sound the same but have different meanings. I think, because the pastor at our church says these words that sound like swear words but aren't really swear words. For example, the pastor at our church will talk about hell from the pulpit. Hell is a real place where unsaved people go to be tormented for the rest of eternity. And it's hot. Not hot like the asphalt basketball courts at the park in town on a 100-degree summer day…but even hotter. So this is hell. But if I say "Oh h@!!," or tell my brother to "go to h@!!," then I will at least get a raised eyebrow, but usually I'll get a soap sandwich. So that's a homonym, right? Two words that sound the same but have different meanings. I can't think of a better example. Both words sound the same, but one word you can say in church and the other gets you in trouble with the potty mouth police.

There is another word. It means donkey in the Bible. I don't know why the author didn't just use the word donkey, but they didn't…in the Bible it is an ass. I say that word flippantly at home and I'm in trouble. But at church it is featured prominently in a Christmas song.

Every Christmas, without fail we will sing "What Child is This." It is a beautiful Old English tune with very powerful lyrics. But I hate the song. Featured prominently in verse number two it says, "Why lies he in such mean estate, while ox and ass are feeding." That's right…there in black is, "While ox and ass are feeding." You can't get around it. Even if you don't say the word, it's still there. And the dozens of people in our little church sing out a swear word that echoes through the rafters.

Every time we start singing that song, I try to prepare myself mentally for the ensuing swear word, but we always sing it and it always make me laugh. I don't know exactly why it's funny, but it is funny to me to hear that word sung at high volume at church.

And every time, my mother is prepared for my laugh. And every time when I laugh, she will flick her finger on the soft spot on my skull. It's really a masterful maneuver. It is subtle, slight and quick, so almost no one at church will notice that a mother is reprimanding her child. But Mom knows exactly where to flick for maximum effect. If I were to choose between a spanking with a wooden spoon and a well-placed flick on the noggin, I'd take the spanking every day.

So this donkey of a curse word gets me into all kinds of trouble. If I say this particular curse word at home, I eat soap. If I don't say this same word at church, but chuckle at forty-four people singing out the same curse word, then I get an even worse reprimand. I guess you could just chalk this up as one of the great mysteries of the English language. You could even chalk it up as one the great mysteries of religion. How a word can be both in the Bible and a curse word? I just don't get it. Is that a homonym or is it a theological conundrum? God only knows.

Dad's arm is not broke. He went to the doctor and got x-rays, but it turned out it's just hurt, not injured. I decided not to tell Mom about the curse word. My Dad had to go to the doctor's office…I consider that punishment enough. He didn't need to suck on a bar of soap too. With his arm banged up, more of the responsibility of training T-bone falls to me. Which is good, I think. I'm the one who has to show him at the fair, so I need to be the one to lead him around at home. I think T-bone is fat and ready for the fair, but Dad tells all of us that they are under weight and need another hundred pounds of finish. So as the fair approaches, we frantically work to get everything ready. Most days, I think to myself, "Oh $#!?, it's about fair time and T-bone and I aren't ready."

I smile quietly, knowing that my mother can't wash my mouth out for my thoughts…otherwise I would use a bar of soap like a lollipop.

Chapter Eight
Butterflies and Lollipops

Do you know that feeling that you get in the pit of your stomach where your guts feel like they are tied in knots? Not like you're going to be sick, just a twisted-up gut. It feels like you swallowed a kaleidoscope of butterflies and they're dancing and twirling in your belly. My Mom says it's just nerves. I heard a p-sycologist on TV one time call it anxiety disorder. I don't think anxiety disorder can kill you, or it would have been a real doctor instead of a p-sycologist on the TV. Regardless of what you want to call it, that butterfly in the belly is real…and the condition persists at the fair.

Even before the fair starts, I get the butterflies. In those quiet moments in the evenings when we're not busy, I have a fleeting thought of T-bone and I picture myself putting him on the truck on Sunday morning after the fair. My stomach gets all twisted up in knots and I try to think about something else. So I think about unloading T-bone at the fair, or the two shows at the fair and my stomach gets tied in knots. It seems like I can't think about anything without my stomach getting nervous. At this point, I try to think about the Double Mint Gum jingle. It is a mindless song that will loop over and over in my mind. With the Double Mint Gum theme playing in my mind, I'm not thinking about anything that makes me nervous.

I am nervous. For the past week, I've been nervous because it's almost fair time. But it is no longer "almost," It is here. Loading them into the trailer is no big deal. We've done that about a dozen times now. But after the steers are loaded, I cram myself into the back seat of my Dad's pickup and I get to worry for the next hour and a half about unloading T-bone in the foreign land known as the fair.

As Dad pulls into the fair, we all pile out of the truck and prepare to unload. Jerry's steer is in the back, so he comes out first. The steer is obviously scared, and why wouldn't he be. He walked into a trailer at our quiet little isolated ranch. He steps out of the trailer in the middle of a big town with thousands of people and all the bustle of the fair. There is dogs barking, mules braying, roosters crowing, pigs squealing, sheep baaing, balloons popping, children on amusement park rides screaming, music playing and the chaotic frivolity of a group of celebrating people.

Jerry stoically reaches through the bars of the trailer and unties his steer. He pulls the lead rope to the back and my Dad swings open the trailer door. Jerry has a terrified look on his face, like a rodeo cowboy when they open the chute gate for the bareback riders. Jerry anchors the lead rope with a half wrap around his hip. Despite all of the anticipation, Jerry's steer casually walks out of the trailer.

Jimmy is next, and, emboldened by Jerry's success, he simply walks in the trailer and walks back out with his steer in tow. The process seems to be getting easier, which bodes well for me.

Next is Laney's steer. Dad won't let Laney get in the trailer, so he climbs in and walks back out. The placid steer stumbles out the trailer door. Dad hands the steer to Laney and Laney glares at me. For the last two years, Dad has led Laney's steer through all of the weigh-in. That is the privileged position of the rookie showman. Now that I'm the rookie, Laney knows that Dad will shepherd me through the process and now she is on her own. So she is mad at me. "What's new," I think to myself.

Most of the time, I can figure out why she is mad at me. I often have to really think about it and unwind the circuitous logic that the female of the species is known for, but I usually figure out the root cause of the injustice that has befallen her. And the root cause typically comes down to me being born. That is certainly the case in this instance.

Dad walks into the trailer and returns leading T-bone. T-bone jumps out of the trailer and spooks. Dad holds him tight and he quickly calms down.

"Get over here and lead your steer, Max," my Dad says. We put the longest lead rope on T-bone, so I know that Dad is going to hold onto the end. But I'm still nervous. A lot can happen before the slack tightens at the anchor. Unlike a boat anchor that is iron and has no social skills, my Dad, as an anchor, will stop and talk to other parents in the steer barn. When my Dad is talking, all of his focus goes to his mouth and ears and he forgets little things like holding onto his son's steer.

Nonetheless, we begin the slow parade through the steer barn. Now the steer barn is a veritable House of Horrors for a steer from a serene barn at our place. First of all, the steer barn is shadowy. Granted, the House of Horrors is completely dark, but for a steer who has naturally poor eye sight, shadowy is just the same as dark. The noises in the steer barn are very similar to the House of Horrors. There are fans blowing and blow dryers humming. There are tack boxes slamming and other steers mooing and bumping into fences. Add that to all of the noise outside the barn and you have a thunderstorm of sounds. A steer has a very refined sense of hearing, so the sounds really are the scariest.

As we wind through the maze of the barn, our first destination is the scales to weigh-in our steers. As we walk along, little kids jump out from all corners. None of them are trying to be scary, but all of them are scary to T-bone. Some of them are just playing with their friends. Others want to pet my steer. That's what the petting zoo is for. I wish someone would carry a sign in front of us that says, "Caution…range steers." None of the kids get kicked, but most of them walk funny. We all wear cowboy boots, so stepping in a cow pie is no big deal. But if you're wearing a thin tennis shoe, or a pair of sandals, squishy cow poop surrounding your bare toes can really ruin your day. The steer barn is one of the few places that we cowboy-boot-wearing people get to reverse traditional roles and make fun of everyone else's foot wear.

The scale is on the far end of the barn right next to our stalls. The process should be pretty simple. The weight scale has a small gate in the front and a small gate in the back, and solid fence on both sides. It is just wide enough for a steer. It has the look and feel of a tipping chute and nothing good happens in the tipping chute. Randy Wainwright's uncle is there to pull on the lead rope and Randy Wainwright's dad is there to push on the rump of every steer. (If you remember, Randy Wainwright is a big kid and it's in his genes.) My Uncle Dan (if you've lost track of my family tree, that's okay. I have a lot of aunts and uncles) works the scale. He slides the counter balance along a slide until the slide balances in the air. He'll look at the tiny engraved numbers and yell out the weight, "ten seventy-five," in this particular situation. "Eleven fifteen," he yells at the next.

The steers have to weigh at least a thousand pounds to enter the fair. My Uncle Dan is typically an honest man, but if a steer is five or ten pounds under weight, Uncle Dan will sneak his toe onto the scale. With a very experienced amount of pressure, Uncle Dan will add the five or ten pounds needed to make weight. While it is technically against the rules, everybody knows about it, but nobody complains. In fact, I think everyone thinks Uncle Dan is a hero instead of a villain in tipping the scales like that. Maybe that's why he is the one always running the scales.

It's finally our turn. Randy Wainwright's uncle pulls on T-bones halter and Randy Wainwright's dad pushes on his tail and rump. T-bone resists, nothing good has ever happened inside a chute. The Wainwright brothers are very persistent and very big, so T-bone reluctantly steps onto the scale. The doors close and T-bone stands patiently for his first test. Uncle Dan balances the scale and I don't see his toe anywhere near the scales. I wait patiently to see if T-bone will make weight.

"Are you worried, Max?" my Uncle Dan asks.

"A little," I reply.

"Ten eighty," Uncle Dan yells out.

I look a little confused, so he reiterates, "One thousand eighty pounds."

My Dad grabs T-bone's halter rope.

"Hang on, Max. I'm just the anchor."

I tentatively wrap my hands around the rope. The gate swings open and T-bone jumps out of the chute. Dad yanks on the rope and T-bone quickly remembers that he is tethered. He gives up and walks dutifully behind me. We walk around a grass covered plaza and back into the barn. The fear in T-bones eyes has waned and we arrive at his stall.

T-bone is intrigued by his new home. There is a bed of straw and a bucket of fetid water. The fairgrounds is notorious for bad water. On our range, there are times that an obnoxious steer will climb into the water trough and whenever a bovine drinks, they will also pee. So after this deviant steer climbs out of the water trough, the rest of the steers must drink this urine fouled water until it clears. This is what the fairgrounds water tastes like. Dad says he can't make coffee strong enough to cover the taste…and Dad is an expert on brewing tongue curling strong coffee.

The straw on the ground is bedding, but to T-bone, it looks more like feed. T-bone drops his head and starts eating the straw.

"Don't let him eat the straw, Max," my Dad tells me. It would have been equally informative for my Dad to say, "Make pigs fly," or "Make fish walk."

"How do I get him to stop?" I ask, trying not to sound whiny, but sounding whiny just the same.

"Tie his head up so he can't reach the straw," my Dad replies.

I tie T-bone's head up high so that he can't eat. I wipe my hands on my pants and start walking away.

"Don't tie him that high, Max," my Dad says. "He can't lie down with his head up that high."

I re-tie T-bone with his rope longer and his head drops to the straw to eat. So I tie his head up a little bit higher.

"Max, I told you to tie his head lower," my Dad sound a little exasperated. I swear my Dad will ignore me and only look when I appear most incompetent.

Jerry comes over and quickly ties up T-bone to save me from more chastising.

We hurriedly put out feed and water. We again hurriedly clean the manure out of the stalls. Steers crap all of the time, and I guess city people don't like the smell so we have to clean it out as soon as it hits the straw.

Still hurrying, we get our tack and feed better organized and then we realize it is late and we have an early morning tomorrow for our first show. We hurry back to the truck where we hurriedly choke down some sandwiches for dinner. This is more hurrying than I am used to.

My grandma lives just up the road from the fairgrounds, so we hurry over to grandma's house to sleep.

"Hurry inside and get to bed," my Dad commands.

I hurry into my pajamas and jump into my sleeping bag, but with all of this hurrying, I can't get to sleep. I should be exhausted and, truth be known, I am. I breathe deeply and keep my eyes closed, but the butterflies keep me distracted from slumber.

I don't know how long it takes, but I finally go to sleep. I hope my restless sleep will be enough to get me through tomorrow.

The judge takes extra long on this class. The Grand Champion round is always competitive and the pressure is high. I masterfully set my steer up with all four feet perfectly placed. I glare at the judge, not angrily, but kind of a John Wayne squint. He stares at me for one more moment. I stare back with a "I-am-your-Grand-Champion" glare. The judge walks over to my steers, extends his hand and...

...starts shaking my shoulder.

"Wake up, Max," I hear my Mom's voice as I open my eyes. "Jump up, it's show day."

"I'm awake," I say unconvincingly. "I'm awake," I say again, this time trying to convince myself.

I roll out of my sleeping bag and rub the sleep out of my eyes. I throw my clothes on and grab a plastic bag full of Apple Jack's cereal. We usually have Cheerios at home, but Grandma spoils us with Apple Jacks.

We all trudge out to the pickup. Mom will come later with the younger kids. Dad fires up the pickup, turns on his headlights and we head to the fairgrounds.

Everything is peaceful at this time in the morning. The fair is still and most everyone is asleep. My Dad parks and the peaceful part of the morning is over. Now is when we hurry.

This is something new and different for my family. My Dad never gets in a hurry. His job mostly entails moving cows and the fastest way to move cows is slow. This laid-back pace spill into everything we do. We're always late, we never rush and we as a family are pretty laid back.

But not this morning. In just a few hours, the show will start and we have a considerable amount to get done in about four hours.

First, we exercise the steers. We take them out to the show ring and walk them in circles. When we finish, we tie the steers up outside the barn. We run back into the barn and fill the steers feed buckets with grain. As the steers eat, we clean the stalls. The straw that the steers lie on is saturated with urine and manure. We use the pitchforks to get as much of the soiled straw out as we can, and then we break open a couple of straw bales and spread it around the stall.

The steers are finished eating, so we take the steers out to the wash racks. As always, washing the steers seems pointless. They enjoy their filth and they will be filthy again…soon. But still, we soap them up with Orvus and then scrub and scrub and scrub. Next, we rinse them off. This step is important because Dad grabs the water hose from me and checks my rinsing work by rinsing T-bone again. I slick all of the water off my steer with the flat, backside edge of a scotch comb.

With T-bone washed and rinsed, I walk a still dripping T-bone back to the stall. I don't feel clean, but I'm dripping too. Back at the stall, I tie T-bone up…not too short, so he can't lie down, and not too long, so he tries to eat the straw. I put out some grass hay for T-bone and he wags his wet tail as he eats.

The next step is agony. The steers have to be completely dry to properly fit them. So they must be blown dry with a special show steer blow dryer. It is about the size of a vacuum cleaner with a ten-foot flexible hose. Out of the nozzle at the end of the hose comes high pressure, warm air. When the steers are wet, you can literally see the water flying off of the hair.

It is a frustratingly tedious process. The blow dryer is a 1980s technology and the electricity in the barn is of a 1940s vintage. Of the 32 blow dryers in the barn, only 26 of them can be used simultaneously without blowing a fuse. And all 32 need to be running to get all of the steers dry before the show. So when the 27th blow dryer is plugged in and turned on, the fuse blows and all of the electricity shuts off. One of the parents will scramble to their tack box and pull out a new fuse. The fuse looks like a flat-topped light bulb. The parent will hastily swap the fuses, the offending plugger of the blow dryer will be chastised for their foolishness, and the blow dryers resume.

"I think T-bone is dry," I tell my Dad.

"He's still wet," he replies with a quick glance in my direction.

Blow dry, blow dry, blow dry.

"I think T-bone is dry," I tell my Dad.

"He's still wet," he replies, this time without the glance.

I can sense he is getting frustrated with me. He has no idea that I am getting frustrated with him.

Blow dry, blow dry, blow dry.

"I think T-bone is dry," I tell my Dad again, emphatically.

"He's still..." this time my Dad is close enough to reach out and touch him. "He's pretty close. Go over him one more time."

Blow dry, blow dry, blow dry.

I turn the dryer off and set it aside, this time without asking.

"What know?" I ask my Dad.

"Show foam him," my Dad hastily replies. He has a pair of scissors in one hand, a bottle of adhesive in the other, and a rag covered in steer manure hanging from his back pocket. I will be the last one to show today, so Dad is focusing on Jerry, Jimmy, and Laney, helping them get ready.

I spray show foam on my steer. It has the consistency of shaving cream or the whipped cream in a can. It is supposed to make their hair frizz out and make them look fatter, but the way I apply it, it just makes him look a little greasy.

"Show foam." I say to myself, making a mental checklist, "check."

"What's next?" I ask my Dad.

"Bone his leg up."

"Bone his legs," I say to myself. I grab a bar of boning wax and a scotch comb. The boning wax looks like a bar of soap, but instead of being slick, it is very sticky. I spread the boning wax on his legs and then comb his hair up. I don't think I'm doing it right, but I'm too stubborn to ask my Dad for help. If done correctly, the boning wax will make the steers legs look thicker and make the steer look more muscular and fatter. The way I do it though, it makes T-bone look like a greaser from the movies.

"Show foam, check. Bone Wax, check"

"What's next?" I ask my Dad.

"Get your mother to do his tail," my Dad replies.

The tail. Now the tail on a normal steer is like a giant fly swatter. Whenever an insect lands on a cow to suck it's blood or lay it's eggs, the bovine's only defense is to switch it's tail and remove the offending insect from it's back. The flexible bones shrouded in leather are quick and agile. There is a stringy mess of hair at the end of the tail. It is this mess of hair that must be "done."

There is a reason that my Dad assigns this task to my Mother. My Mom went to high school and college in the humid south in the 1960s. Bouffant and bee hive hair dos where popular and she would tease here hair up into a big bee hive. She would slather on AquaNet hairspray to keep it from wilting in the Southern heat and humidity.

In my Dad's twisted mind, the ball that must be crafted at the end of the steers tail resembles my mother's bouffant hairstyle. So she is the tail master.

Now, my Dad loves cattle…all things cattle. But my mother has less of an affinity for the bovine species. Cattle are by nature disgusting creatures. They belch all the time. They kick dirt on themselves. They lay in their own manure. And the worst comes from their hind end. If they're not farting, then they are pooping. And they can shoot it out like a missile.

A couple of years ago, my mother was reluctantly putting a tail up in a ball when the steer began to protest. One way that we get the steers to move is to give their tail a slight twist. It's a twinge of pain that a steer will walk away from. So this particular steer mistook my mother handling his tail for the all-too-familiar tail twist. But because he was tied to the wall of the barn, he had nowhere to go. He just danced to the left and the right. In his dancing, he stepped on my mother's foot.

Now, everyone that has been anywhere near cattle can tell you the most painful occurrence is to be kicked by a cow. The second most painful is to be stepped on. Your foot will turn black and you'll have trouble walking for a couple of days. Because of this incident, my mother does all of her work stooped over, and with her arm extended as far as possible. She is not going to be stepped on again. Also, because of this incident, my mother is in a foul mood whenever she encounters the tail end of a bovine.

"Keep him still, Max," my Mother implores with an exasperated glare.

I scratch his back. I doubt my efforts are working, but the theater of me doing something keeps my mother from yelling at me.

"Get a pitchfork and clean up this poop," my mother scolds me. "You're cleaning my boots if I get any on them."

I scurry with the urgency of fear. I think my mother is being unreasonable…but unreasonable is a mother's prerogative.

"I need another zip tie, Max," my Mother is well beyond asking please.

"Where are the zip ties?" I ask.

"I don't know. Just find them," my Mother says with a black comb in her teeth. She has run out of hands and the comb in her teeth only raises her ire.

I run to the tack box. It is a mess from all of the preparations for the day. Paper towels, show foam, Orvus. I dig through the tack box. Safety pins, combs, brushes, show halters, zip ties. Zip ties! I grab the zip ties and then throw everything haphazardly back into the tack box.

"Hurry, Max, or I'll lose it and have to start over."

I run to the stall, taking special precautions to slow down when I get close so I don't scare T-bone. But still fast enough that I don't get yelled at for being slow.

My mother puts the finishing touches on her perfect tail ball and then picks up the spray can of tail adhesive and starts spraying. It looks like a lot of adhesive, but I don't want to question her methods. In fact, I don't want to interact verbally in any way. I just want to get done.

"He's close," my Mom says. "Go change your clothes…and make sure your boots are clean."

With a sense of relief, I walk back to the tack box. I grab my show clothes and head to the changing room. My show clothes are really nothing special. They are just my regular clothes, only new. I can't overemphasize the risk I'm taking in wearing show clothes. Because they are new, there are no imperceptible stains or other minute imperfections that my mother would classify as ruined. My show clothes, once on, aren't going to church or school pictures, or some other controlled environment. I am going to the barn, with dirt, dust, manure, slobber, and 1,478 other foreign substances that will "ruin" my brand-new clothes. I have mentally prepared myself for my mother's chastisement because getting dirty is inevitable.

I thread my fancy belt through my impeccable belt loops and gather my grubby clothes to head back to the tack room. My mother notices a smudge of dust on the knee of my show clothes.

"Max," I look up with puppy dog eyes. I've learned a smile doesn't work. "You have to show in those pants," she says as she aggressively brushes the offending dust from my pants. I'm looking forward to the next tail she needs to put up.

"Max," my Dad calls out. "We need to head to the show ring."

I throw my hat on and grab my show stick and show comb. It's all happening so fast now. I'm nervous and I can't seem to calm down. Fortunately, the junior show steer world has a veritable cornucopia of remedies for antsy steers.

There are three broad categories of steer relaxants: pharmacological, herbal, and pantry. These three broad categories can be broken down even further.

There are the pharmacological remedies. Veterinarians have injections and pills that can be used to calm or sedate a horse. If they use it on a steer, it is called "off label" use. I think "off label" is just a legal way of saying, "we're not supposed to use this, but it works and we went to 8 years of school so we can get away with it."

Dad says that it is unethical and against the rules so we don't use pharmaceuticals, which is convincing and logical. He also says that whoever ends up eating those steaks will lose feeling in their lips and tongues. That seems less convincing, but I like to picture the banquet where everyone has lost sensation in their lips and tongue. Imagine the conversation. Imagine the keynote speaker. "I can't feel my thongue."

The next category of magical steers elixirs are herbals or hippie remedies. Dad says these are legal, ethical, non-controversial, and completely ineffective. That is why we use them. Melatonin, mentholatum, yarrow leaves, chamomile tea, and lavender oil are used to equal effect. Dad prefers lavender oil. He says it makes him smell like an old lady.

Typically, the herbals are placed on their nose or put on their feed or water. Dad will slather lavender oil all over his hand and then rubs his hand on the steer's nose. Then he will use that same hand to wipe the steers butt before the steer goes in the show ring. And then he'll use that same hand to eat a cheeseburger right after the show. And he always complains that his cheeseburger tastes funny.

The last category of steer relaxants are what I term the pantry remedies. Pick an edible household item…any household item, and feed it to your steer. Sugar cubes, Hersey chocolate, Gatorade, or a six pack of beer.

The Wainwrights use the beer trick. It's really pretty simple. Mr. Wainwright would spend all morning scurrying around, barking orders and leaving behind a trail of chaos and nervousness. His wife would get anxious, his kids would get anxious, and the steers would get anxious. It's a good thing that Randy is a big kid, or his steer would drag him all over the show ring.

So to calm the steers, Mr. Wainwright would pour a six pack of beer in their water. It really doesn't do anything like you might think. Steers naturally brew alcohol in their own stomach. It's probably more than a six-pack worth, but a steer metabolizes the alcohol so it doesn't make them goofier than they already are.

This year, Mr. Wainwright is trying something different. Instead of giving the beer to the steers, he is drinking the beer. This has proven to be the most effective steer calm treatment. The beer calms Mr. Wainwright down. With Mr. Wainwright calm, Mrs. Wainwright and all of the Wainwright boys are calm. With all of the Wainwright boys calm, all of their steers stand placidly chewing their cud without a care in the world.

The lavender oil doesn't seem to be working. T-bone is nervous and so am I. I try deep breathing. I try relaxation. I try self-hypnosis, but nothing seems to work. I resign myself to the fact that I will be nervous for the show. Butterflies reign.

I walk slowly into the show ring with T-bone in tow. He steps out proudly and I hold his head up high. We are in the middle of the class with three steers in front of us and four steers behind. The judge stands in the center of the ring. He wears freshly pressed khaki slacks, a fancy light blue shirt and a red tie. His flawless grey cowboy hat is pulled low and I can see him squint behind his aviator sunglasses. He looks seriously and I squint seriously back at him.

The steers, led by their showmen, line up side by side in a neatly curated row. The judge walks in front of the steers and each showman, including me, does a silly little dance with the judge as he passes. I make sure T-bone's feet are set properly and then I scratch his belly with my show stick. T-bone switches between chewing his cud and licking my shirt. His drool and cud are all over my brand-new shirt, and it is most certainly ruined.

The next phase of the show, the judge touches each steer. This seems creepy and pointless to me, but supposedly, with this magic touch, the judge can tell how much fat they have and how big their ribeye is.

The judge walks down the line, touching each steer, and then, as the judge walks away, the showman will pull a special comb out of his back pocket and comb the disturbed hair back into place. With as much show foam as we put on his hair, it will take more than a gentle touch, but all of the showmen comb their steers after the judge turns away…but close enough that he can still see you, so you can get credit for it, but still far enough away that he can't see you. Like everything else in my life, it's very confusing. But Dad said to do it, so I'll do it…that's not confusing.

Finally, the judge walks up to T-bone. I grip my halter tightly and gently scratch T-bone on the brisket with my showstick. The judge places his hand on his ribs, and then reaches up to T-bone's back. As the judge reaches for T-bone's back, I remember a bit from my science class. Thousands of years ago, prey species would be attacked from the skies by pterodactyls and other flying dinosaurs. This constant threat from the skies will make most prey mammals crouch slightly whenever a shadow passes over them. Humans today will even duck when a shadow passes over them based on the instincts from our Neanderthal ancestors. Randy Wainwright will crouch even lower because his Neanderthal ancestors are more prevalent in his family tree.

Even more prescient for a bovine, the most effective means for a mountain lion to kill its prey is to jump on the prey's back and bite and severe it's spinal cord. This is all a lengthy and wordy way of saying, "steers might not like being touched on their back."

As the judge reaches for T-bones back, a thousand years of instinct courses through T-bone's brain, spine, and various other synapses. T-bone reflexively picks his leg up and kicks the judge.

Now, I have to give credit to T-bone for his aim. Another well-known scientific fact is that there is a location on the male of the human species which has over a thousand nerve endings. This location is completely unprotected by bone or muscle and lies directly between his legs. That's right, T-bone nailed the judge right in the Oscar Mayer wiener. Got him right in his twig and berries. Hit him right in the…well, you get the picture.

The judge doubles over in pain. He tries to pretend that he's not hurt, but every male who has taken a soft ball to the tenders knows he is in pain. His hat is askew on the side of his head and his sun glasses are knocked to the ground.

I stand there, not sure what to do. I know I'm supposed to comb T-bone's hair back into place, but I'm not sure what the protocol is. Do I wait until the judge's testicles descend? Or at least wait until he gets up off the grass? That's what I'll do, once he gets up.

The judge grabs his glasses, but doesn't adjust his hat. He will judge the rest of my show with his hat off kilter. As he steps away, I pull out my comb and comb T-bone's hair forward, just like my Dad showed me. T-bone stands there, perfectly set up. I think things are going pretty good. The judge's complexion has gone from tan to white to green.

The judge walks gingerly to the other side of the ring and circles his hand. Everyone in the class takes two steps forward and then we start a head to tail procession, along the arc of the fence. We continue our parade until we are on the other side of the ring standing head to tail.

The time is getting short and it is critical for everything to go right now. T-bone perfectly steps into his feet being set up. I just have to poke his front foot with my showstick, and he is set. I take a deep breath and train my eye on the judge. Without hesitation, he points at me first. Before he has a chance to change his mind, I gather my showstick and walk to the first position. The rest of the class will line up beside me.

I confidently scratch T-bones belly. The rest of the placing goes pretty quickly. Second place, third place, fourth place line up next to me. I try to contain my excitement as I scratch T-bone's belly. T-bone stands easily, chewing his cud.

The judge takes the longest time placing the last place steer and second to last. He asks them to walk in a small circle. He asks them some questions. And then he finally places them last and second to last.

The judge strides to the microphone at the edge of the arena…hat still askew and green hoof print on his crotch. He clicks on the microphone and it squeals with feedback. He clears his throat to explain his decision.

"This is a real tough class," the judge says. He says that about every class. "The little girl in first does a real good job with her Angus steer."

Wait…What? I'm not a girl. I look to the end of the line. The ring steward is handing the girl a first-place trophy and she leads her steer out of the show ring. The steward then hands a second-place trophy to the next boy in line. So if that end is first place, then I am…dead last. I am proud of how well T-bone did. It must have been something that I did.

With the rest of the class exiting before me, I finally leave the show ring. T-bone seems oblivious to the fact that we lost. In reality, he *is* oblivious. He is excited at the prospect of a fresh flake of hay.

I can't believe I lost. I know it's a bad idea, but I'll ask Dad what went wrong.

"What happened?" I ask. "What went wrong? I didn't think I did that bad."

"It's pretty hard to overcome your steer kicking the judge in the gonads."

"You think he's sore about that."

"He's sore alright. I don't think he could, in good conscience, place you any higher than he did. He has his pride to think about."

I'm not sure that it's fair, I mean, how am I supposed to keep T-bone from kicking? And how could I know that he had such good aim? Who knows?

Stripping all of the adhesives out of a steer's hair is almost as much work as putting it in. I spray him with Aftershow and then we lead him out to the wash rack. I douse him with a bucket of Purple Oil and then another bucket of Orvus soap and water. I scrub the soap into his hair with the same vigor I did this morning. I'm told that if I don't get all of the adhesive out, then my fitting job won't look quite as good tomorrow. I think our general lack of knowledge on how to competently fit a show steer is a bigger impediment than some residual adhesive. Just the same, I do my best to get T-bone clean. It's almost hot out this afternoon, so T-bone enjoys his bath more than he did in the chilly morning.

As I work, I look down and remember that I'm still wearing my show clothes. A chill runs down my spine as I remember my mother telling all of us, "be sure to change back into your grubby clothes. You have to wear your show clothes next week to school."

I look down, and to my horror, I have black adhesive all over my shirt. *It's ruined,* I think to myself. As if today couldn't get any worse. I have painted black spots all over my fancy white shirt. I shake my head and say a discouraging word under my breath. I hurry and rinse T-bone and walk back to the stall. Should I hurry and change it and let Mom find out about it when she does laundry? It will be a few days from now because Mom doesn't have access to a washer and dryer at the fair. And doing fair laundry puts her in a foul mood anyway. I decide to wear my mess proudly and take the lecture today.

"Max," my mother yells from across the barn. I know I say that my Mom yells a lot, and it's probably a little unfair. There are other mothers at the fair that actually yell at their kids and makes my mother's yells seem much more quiet and non-threatening. But a yell is what I hear, and I will keep saying yell for dramatic effect, if nothing else.

"Max," my mother yells, "what is on your shirt?"

I look down at my shirt, knowing what is there. I glance back up in feigned disbelief, "I don't know what that is," I lie.

"I thought I told you to change into your grubby clothes before going to the wash rack," my mother exclaims.

"I guess I forgot," I reply, and that is the truth.

"You are supposed to wear that shirt to school next week," she reminds me. My mother has already started untucking my shirt. She hastily unbuttons my shirt, a task that I'm obviously incapable of, and pulls the shirt from my back. I stand in the aisle of the steer barn naked from the waist up, because my mother would rather me be naked than wear a ruined shirt.

Every child that has grown up in the record playing generation understands the concept of a record skip. Instead of listening to a digital download of music on a match box sized electronic device, or some futuristic method of listening to music pumped directly into your brain through your pinky finger from a device the size of a grain of rice…we listened to records.

A record was a little like a CD or DVD, but was a vinyl disk that an armature would follow in a circular groove reading a series of bumps that would vibrate a disk called a speaker, creating sound waves and high-fidelity music. It is really an ingenious system that worked without flaw, unless the vinyl record obtained a scratch.

A scratch on a record was typically the result of me or one of my brothers horsing around when we were holding the record. No one really knows exactly how it happens, dropping it will break the disk, but just the wrong movement will scratch that disk. The scratch will cause the armature to make an eerie screech and then the armature will skip, always back on the record. The result is…you'll be listening to your favorite Marty Robbins song and it will suddenly chirp and repeat the last four stanzas, and then skip again at the same spot. Your favorite record will continue to skip at the same place over and over into perpetuity unless you pick up the armature and physically move it past the skip. It becomes so indelible that when you hear the song on the radio, it will sound strange when it doesn't skip over and over again.

So what's the point of a skip? Well, the fair is very similar to a skipping record. I have reached the point in the fair that it plays over and over again until someone moves the armature. The next day at the fair is exactly the same. The name of the show is different, but the early morning is the same, feeding is the same, the time at the wash rack, the fitting, the showing, and the red ribbon is the same. The judge is judging how T-bone is put together instead of how I am showing, but the result is the same.

But with the second show over, the stress of the fair has melted away and the fun of the fair is just getting started.

102

Chapter Nine
Reverse Peristaltic Action
(The Barf Chapter)

Warning: This chapter is about vomit. If you have a weak stomach or a strong gag reflex, you should consider skipping to Chapter 10.

Reverse peristaltic action is a very scientific way of describing a very common bodily function that most children are familiar with. Reverse peristaltic action is an involuntary response to digestive disruption. It occurs when a person gets a stomach virus or bacteria, or food poisoning of some type. The toxins in the digestive tract must be eliminated before it circulates through the rest of the body. There is a small flap of tissue where the esophagus meets the stomach. This flap of tissue, called the epiglottis, allows chewed and swallowed food to enter the stomach, but it folds back into place to prevent your sloshing digesta from splashing out of the stomach. In the case of reverse peristaltic action, the epiglottis will fold down, creating an opening for the stomach contents.

Peristaltic action is the smooth muscle movements that push your food and digesta through the gastro-intestinal tract. Swallowing is peristaltic action. That grumble in your tummy is peristaltic action moving your digesta through your intestines and colon.

With reverse peristaltic action, that motion involuntarily reverses. With the epiglottis open and the smooth muscle flexing in reverse, the contents of your stomach will flow up your esophagus, out your mouth and onto your brand-new shoes.

Reverse peristaltic action is barf, puke, spew, upchuck, vomit, ralph, erp, blow chunks, toss your cookies, lose your lunch, to be sick, regurgitation, and yak…to name a few of the innumerable descriptions.

There is a variety of triggers for reverse peristaltic action. In addition to the aforementioned viruses, bacterium, and toxins, there are two other triggers that are prevalent at the fair…overeating and motion sickness.

The explanation for overeating is pretty simple. You eat too much, your digestive system can't work fast enough to move it along, then some simple jostling of your stomach and everything flips into reverse and you throw up in the parking lot of North's Chuckwagon Buffet.

My brother Jerry has a love/hate relationship with all-you-can-eat buffets generally and North's Chuckwagon Buffet specifically. For most people, all-you-can-eat is a humble invitation. For Jerry, all-you-can-eat is a personal challenge.

"All-I-can-eat?" Jerry always asks when we walk into the dining room.

"It's all-you-can-comfortably-eat," my mother always implores. She's the one who has to clean up Jerry's messes, so she always tries, unsuccessfully, to get Jerry to moderate.

"I just want to get my monies worth…$7 worth of food," Jerry explains.

Jerry shovels in the food. He has ribs, next to lasagna, beside a pile of nachos. He doesn't just over eat, he over eats with blind abandon to the richness of the foods and how they may interact with each other.

There is a fountain of chocolate with germs of dozens of other people that you can dip strawberries and rice crispies treats in. Not Jerry. He dips brownies in the chocolate, and chocolate chip cookies, and the other desserts that don't require added chocolate. One time, I saw Jerry diving toward the chocolate fountain with his mouth wide open. Before he could stick his head under the chocolate fountain and drink chocolate until his heart stops, my mother flicked him in the soft spot on his skull. He rubbed the spot and complained about the discipline, but my mother most certainly saved his life.

At the buffet, there is a gluttonous monument to binging, more commonly called the soft serve ice cream machine. My grandma always tells us that ice cream is the perfect dessert, because it slides between the cracks. Mom, again being the one who cleans up the mess, disagrees with that sentiment and has plenty of evidence to the contrary. But there is Jerry, piling the soft serve ice cream high into the special little serving dish.

And soft serve ice cream is perhaps the worst dessert for tipping someone over the edge. Soft serve ice cream goes from yummy dessert into gross melty milky mess in about two minutes, so you have just less than two minutes to eat it.

Jerry will always shovel that last bite into his mouth, wipe it with his napkin and smile a satisfied smile. But that smile last for a two count as his overworked stomach begins to revolt.

Jerry will swallow hard. He'll get up and go to the bathroom.

"I'm gonna make some more room," he always says, knowing that sneaking a little bit out the backdoor never helps.

Jerry will lie down on a bench, but without the aid of gravity, his lunch sloshes upward. He quickly sits back up and the sudden movement makes it worse.

Dad, seeing his discomfort, asks, "Jerry, do you need to go to the restroom?"

"I've already been," Jerry replies, not quite getting what Dad is really asking.

"Let's head out to the car," Dad commands, hoping to avoid a scene in the lobby.

Everyone gives Jerry a wide berth. Much like Mt. St. Helens, Jerry could blow at any moment. Jerry gets about half way through the parking lot and his shoulders heave. Jerry struggles to keep his lunch down, but we all see this tell-tale sign pointing to the inevitable spew.

"Don't look, Max," my Dad yells at me. Everyone knows about my weak stomach and quick gag reflex. It's good advice, but it's the sight and sound and smell working in concert that get me. I avert my eyes, in the hopes I don't participate in Jerry's upchuck party.

…And thar she blows.

In a quick instance, seven dollars and forty-five minutes of gluttony spill out onto the parking lot. I feel sorry for the good people walking into North's Chuckwagon, preparing themselves for an enjoyable homestyle meal. They stare horrified at the display in the parking lot.

Was this poor boy ill…Is it contagious? Was it something he ate? Will we be eating the same thing? The line of questioning from the poor folks could be endless.

As the people walking into the restaurant quickly do a risk analysis on the safety of eating at this locale, we are loading up and leaving the scene of the crime. That is the best example of the over eating digestive upset.

Motion sickness is the second type and is a little bit different. Inside your inner ear are a series of micro-cilia. Micro-cilia could better be described as tiny little hairs. There is fluid around the hairs and when you move, fluid moves the cilia. Your brain uses the moving micro-cilia and visual stimuli to control your balance. It is really an ingenious system that keeps us from falling on our face.

But when there is a difference between what the micro-cilia is telling the brain, and what your eyes are telling your brain, the whole balance system goes haywire. In what could only be described as an evolutionary mystery, when your balance system goes haywire, your body will feel the need to eliminate your stomach contents. This is referred to as nausea and the end result, especially in children is a full out upchuck.

So what does all of this disgusting narrative have to with the fair? The fair involves both over eating and nausea…so the reverse peristaltic action is inevitable.

T-bone and most of the other steers lie in their straw covered stalls. They do what steers usually do…chew their cud. I sit next to T-bone, trying to spend as much time as I can in the remaining days we have together. It seems like what I should do, but T-bone isn't much of a conversationalist, so I'm getting bored.

"Hey Max," Benny hollers from across our corner of the barn.

"Hey Benny," I reply in my most melancholy voice.

"What's got you down?" Benny asks.

"I don't know," I reply, which is the truth.

I am like most other twelve-year-olds. I have all of these feelings and emotions, but I don't always know what to call them and I don't always know what to do with them.

"Why don't we hit the midway?" Benny says. That really is his solution for everything at the fair. You just got stepped on…let's go the midway. You just won grand champion…let's go to the midway. You just got last place…let's go to the midway.

The midway at the fair is the geographic and cultural center of the fair. It is an open space covered in grass that stretches from the livestock barns on the North to the parking lot on the South. To either side of the midway is the rodeo arena, merchants buildings, the free stage, the home arts building, and the RV park where everybody else stays during the week.

But in the center, the midway is home to the food vendors on the north following right into the carnival rides to the south.

We start with the food vendors. We start at the Shriners Booth for a hamburger. We get nachos at the 4-H food booth. Lonnie Walker's aunt makes pies for the Baptist booth and we wouldn't want to hurt her feelings, so we stop for pie. Next is ice cream at the Buhl FFA booth followed by a Pepsi from the Knights of Columbus. No fair would be complete without a burrito from the Guadalupe Center booth. I feel a little bit like Jerry at a buffet. We skip the high brow places like the Buhl Catholic Church booth. They sell fried trout and none of us can afford it. And my family always eats at the Tater Pig place on Saturday night before the rodeo. The last stop is in that transition zone between the food vendors and the carnival. This is where the traveling food vendors are housed. There are part of the carnival and are professionals. There is a corn dog booth, a caramel apple booth, and a cotton candy booth. We stop for a fluff of cotton candy.

It amazes me how much a twelve-year-old can eat. We walk around, to let our stomachs settle, but you just read what we ate…there's no way it will settle. Against our better judgement, we walk over to the ticket booth to get our P.O.P pass. The P.O.P pass is an acronym for "Pay-One-Price." You pay twenty dollars and they stamp a P.O.P. stamp on your hand and all you have to do is show the toothless carnival worker your stamp and they let you onto any ride as many times as you want. Only suckers buy tickets.

I pay the twenty dollars and get the stamp. Randy and Benny each chip in ten dollars. Benny gets the stamp, quickly turns around, and licks the back of his hand where the stamp lies. The moisture prevents the ink from drying and makes the back of his hand a P.O.P. stamp. Benny gets out of sight from the ticket booth, and then presses the back of his hand to the back of Randy's hand. The wet ink sticks to Randy's hand and just like that, Randy and Benny get a buy-one-steal-one-free.

In retrospect, not only is Benny and Randy's scheme illegal, it's also disgusting. That stamp has been pressed on thousands of hands and has never been cleaned. That alone is pretty disgusting, but what makes it worse is Benny licking that stamp. I'm guessing that Benny's got a pretty strong immune system. If he didn't, he would surely be dead by now.

Armed with our freshly dried P.O.P., we head into the chaos of the carnival. There is stimuli everywhere. All of the rides have lights everywhere. During the afternoon, it's not quite as bright, but it's still pretty impressive. Each ride has its own soundtrack. The Ferris Wheel has a calliope playing over its loud speakers. The Rock-O-Planes and the Zipper both play rock and roll music. All of the music mixes together with a thousand conversations for a symphony of noise.

We stand at the Tilt-O-Whirl. The Tilt-O-Whirl is a series of egg-shaped cars that pivot around a center point as all of the center points rotate and rise and fall. The rotation with the rising and falling causes the car to spin around its axis. Everyone knows that the funnest kid to go on the Tilt-O-Whirl with is Randy Wainwright. It doesn't necessarily need to be Randy, but Randy is fifty pounds heavier than anyone else in our crew. With the offset weight balance, the centrifugal force is isolated like tying a rock to the end of a string and spinning it. And with Randy Wainwright in one seat of the car, the ride will spend two and a half minutes spinning like a tornado.

I opt to ride with Lucas Grainger and Mickey Logan. Benny rides with Randy. The spinning really churns my stomach up. I shouldn't have eaten that cotton candy. But I don't want to admit any weakness to my friends so we bound down the stairs of the Tilt-O-Whirl and sashay to the Rock-O-Planes. If a ride has an "O" in the middle of it, you should expect to spin in two directions. The Rock-O-Planes is basically a Ferris Wheel that has a caged gondola that will spin in circles. The spinning is controlled by a steering like wheel. When you spin this wheel, the cage will spin.

I refuse to ride with Benny. Benny will spin the wheel like a mad man, and my stomach is still just a little bit off. I can see that Randy is a little queasy, too. So I jump in a cage with him.

"Go easy, Randy," I say, "my stomach is still a little off."

"Good idea, Max," he replies.

Randy holds the wheel still so the ride acts more like a Ferris Wheel. Benny is just in front of us. So as we go around, he is right behind us, right above us, right in front of us, and right below us as we go around and around. Benny's hands are moving as fast as they can. Lucas closes his eyes. He looks like he wants to scream, but I think he's afraid of opening his mouth. Around and around we spin for two and a half minutes.

My stomach looks up at me, as if to say, "If this is a strategy to help me digest the junk food feast from earlier, it's not working."

I take a deep breath as the Rock-O-Planes slow to a stop. Lucas is as white as a sheet. Benny has a maniacal grin on his face. I'm not sure if he is enjoying the ride, or enjoying the nausea he has inflicted on Lucas.

As we exit the ride, I see an unoccupied bench. I quickly move to the bench and sit down.

"I think I'm gonna ride this ride for a minute," I tell my friends.

"What ride?" Benny asks. Benny doesn't handle nuance very well.

"The bench, Benny," I reply. "I'm gonna lose my lunch if I don't settle my stomach for a second."

"But if we don't keep moving, we'll never ride enough rides to cover the cost of the P.O.P."

How can you argue with Benny's logic? I didn't at the time, but the best argument would have been, you only paid ten dollars for your pass and if you figure the cost of tickets, you'll break even on your fourth ride. And you'll waste the twenty dollars in food that we just ate. But I didn't make that argument…I jumped up and followed our Pied Piper…Benny.

"What do you wanna ride next?" Randy asks.

"How about the Ferris Wheel," I suggest, hoping for a calm ride.

"The Ferris Wheel is for sissy's," Benny pronounces, "Let's go on the Magic Carpet Ride."

Ahhh….the Magic Carpet Ride. It's really a pretty simple ride. It has a series of eight cars on a circular platform. The cars swing in and out, and after the ride starts spinning, a massive hydraulic ram pushes the platform up so it's at a 45-degree angle. All while still spinning.

There is no wheel that controls how fast it spins, so I jump into the seat next to Benny. Lucas looks a little bit off, but he jumps into the car next to Randy.

The operator of the ride pinches the burning end of his cigarette and places it behind his ear so he can relight it after the ride. The operator goes through a rigorous checklist of safety features. The checklist actually has one item to check…make sure the safety bar is latched. I double check his work, because I care more about my life than he seems to. We're already settled in and Benny still has that weird look on his face, which I think means he's having fun. Lucas looks back to Benny from the car in front of us. He looks a little scared, I think, but I'm not very good at judging emotion.

Over the load speaker plays a song that sounds like an American band imitating an Arabian band. The operator moves to the controls, takes a sip of his Coca-Cola to help him get through the day, and then flips the switch.

The car that Benny and I are in lurches forward. The ride spins what seems faster than it's actually going. I see the fair spinning around me. After about a dozen spins, it's impossible to count, the hydraulic ram pushes the still spinning ride up to the 45-degree angle. With a settled stomach, this is where the ride gets fun. The cars, or magic carpets swing from side to side as they spin at this new angle. But this new angle is just enough to tip Lucas's nausea over the edge. Benny and I can't see Lucas throw up, but we quickly know he has. Lucas's stomach contents spew behind him and splatter all over Benny and I.

I don't care how strong your stomach is, if you get it on you, it will gross you out and you will blow chunks. Benny leans over his edge. I barf between my legs. We're at the top of the circle, so as Benny's stomach empties, Randy can see it dribbling to the center of the ride. An unbelievable buffet of hamburger, pie, nachos, ice cream, and cotton candy are quickly added to the center of the ride. The other kids on the ride are equally nauseas and have had a similar diet. Four other kids upchuck their lunch also. The operator has awakened from his routine and has shut the ride down. But the inertia of the ride spins another six spins and twenty seconds to level back out. Two more kids toss their cookies in the interim.

I never like to admit it, but I always feel better after I throw up. It's as if my stomach calls a truce after expelling the offending contents. Benny seems unfazed, Randy barely notices, and Lucas is embarrassed at starting the spew fest. This is one instance where being a trend setter isn't a good thing.

We all exit the ride and the carnival worker leaps into action. He has a 25-pound bag of what could best be described as puke crystals. It looks like kitty litter and smells like bananas. These magic crystals absorb the liquid and, more importantly, the smell. The carnival worker sweeps up the crystals and places them in a garbage can next to his controls. It is apparent that this is a regular part of the job.

I'm a little bit skeptical that their health and hygiene protocols are up to par, but they seem okay with it and, equally important, the next customers are more than willing to jump onto the Magic Carpet Ride and try their luck.

We climb off the Magic Carpet Ride and that bench that we passed up seems very inviting. We sit quietly, not sure what to say.

"Sorry," Lucas says.

His apology seems a little out of place. We should probably be apologizing to him for our fair food smorgasbord followed by spinning in circles until he threw up. I guess we're all to blame.

But we still have P.O.P. stamped on our hand, and we're all feeling better, so we head back to the rides.

We all smell a little funky, but so does everybody else. We ride the Ferris Wheel, just to get our sea legs back. We run the Bumper Cars, and after the two calm rides, we're ready for the good rides again. We ride the Zipper, and then the Spyder. We have to ride the Tilt-O-Whirl again because everyone in our group wants to ride the Tilt-O-Whirl with Randy. We ride the Roller Coaster, and we're disappointed because it's a super small roller coaster. As part of a travelling carnival, it has to be small enough to fit on a road legal truck.

We go through the Fun House a couple of times. My favorite part is the funny mirrors. The funny mirrors are concave or convex mirrors that reflect the image back in funny ways. One mirror makes Randy look super tall and skinny. Another mirror makes Benny look as round as a bowling ball. I don't look all that funny in the mirrors, but everyone else does.

We spend the rest of the afternoon spinning and flying through the air. We twist and climb and fall and spin and then we do it all again. As the sun hangs low in the West, we all head back to the steer barn to feed. The spew fest that started the afternoon is all but forgotten at this point. Except that everyone is hungry and no one has any money.

Back at the barn, T-bone lies in his stall, chewing his cud. I know that I have used this "chewing his cud" phrase throughout this book, but I haven't really explained it. I think the barf chapter is a very appropriate place for a description.

We already established that cattle are prey animals. This means that they must develop survival strategies to minimize their exposure to predators.

When a cow grazes, they are vulnerable to predation. And because they eat forage and other feed that lack nutrient density, they have to eat a lot of roughage every day. So when they graze, they will eat and swallow as much grass as they can. All of the grass goes straight to the rumen. The cow will graze until the rumen is really full…all without chewing their food.

Now, I don't know about you, but whenever I eat too fast, my mother will yell at me, "slow down and chew your food."

T-bone's mother would tell him just the opposite. "Mooooo," she would yell to T-bone, which could be loosely translated as, "hurry up and eat, stop chewing your food."

So with his belly full, the bovine will find a place to lie down. It will provide some cover so they can't be seen by predators, and preferably a shady spot. Once lying down, the cow will begin chewing its cud.

So first, the rumen will form mouth sized balls. From the rumen, these balls, or boluses, will return to the reticulum, and then back up the esophagus to the mouth. This process is called regurgitation. With a bolus regurgitated into their mouth, the cow will use their back teeth to masticate, or chew, their feed.

Once the feed is sufficiently broken up with the cow's teeth, it will swallow the bolus and the reticulum will regurgitate another bolus up the esophagus into the mouth and start the whole process over again. A bovine will typically spend twice as long chewing their cud as they do actually grazing. And they spend most of their day grazing. That is really all a cow does all day. Either grazing or chewing their cud. It doesn't leave very much time for school work, or sports, or entertainment. But that's okay, because entertainment for a cow consists entirely of chewing it cud.

And that is where I find T-bone. He lies down in his stall as his teeth and jaws works over a bolus of cud. His lower jaw waggles from side to side, his eyes are partially closed and his ears are comfortably pulled back. As he chews, he throws his head back to his shoulder to shoo away some flies.

"Hey T-bone," I say as I check on his water bucket.

It's slightly less than half way and has grain and straw floating in it so I freshen it up with a new bucket.

I hesitate, just to see if T-bone wants to talk, and when it's obvious that he doesn't, I return to my friends. T-bone is enjoying a good cud chewing with his buddies, and I'll go find some mischief with my buddies.

Chapter Ten
Fishing for Fools

Every family has a favorite holiday. For some families, it's Christmas, other prefer Easter. Some families go all out on Independence Day, nearly burning down the neighborhood with fireworks and Barbeque. Some families will turn their house into a haunted house for Halloween. In my family, we go all out for April Fools Day.

April Fools Day is a holiday with a long tradition in my family. We will spend months preparing for April Fools Day. One year, my Dad grew a beard for four months just for an April Fools Day prank.

There are a full range of pranks, too. Jerry uses the same April Fools joke every year. He will put crumpled up paper or a handful of dog food in everybody's boots. It's not really much of a prank, more of an annoyance. Everyone dumps out Jerry's April Fool, pulls on their boots and gets on with their day.

Laney is considerably meaner with her pranks. She will put tacks on chairs for people to sit on. She will put honey in her brothers' socks. She will put saw dust or glitter in our shoes. Mom had to ban glitter a few years ago because she ultimately had to clean up the mess. I've heard a television commercial say that "diamonds are forever." I don't know if that's true or not, but I know that glitter mess is forever.

My Mom always has the best April Fools joke. One year she made chocolate chip pancakes for breakfast. But instead of chocolate chips, she used raisins. They were pretty good, but when you're expecting chocolate, raisins don't quite cut it.

Another year she baked a cake with a cup and a half of salt and a table spoon of sugar. The regular recipe calls for a cup and a half of sugar and a tablespoon of salt. That is a big change and there is nothing yummy about salty cake.

The funny thing about Mom, is she doesn't need to watch and she never yells out, "April Fools." She knows that her pranks are effective and she will laugh quietly to herself just knowing that her children are biting into salty cake.

I've heard of some great pranks. Some people will put plastic wrap on a toilet seat. That gets messier than I want to contend with. I've heard of a prank where you put Kool Aid in the shower faucet. This ends with someone covered in red water, but it requires plumbing skills…which I lack.

The best one I pulled off got me into pretty big trouble. I took Laney's bottle of shampoo and filled it with hand lotion. Laney's hair was super greasy for a week after…which was funny. Except Easter was three days later, and we took family photos with Laney and her super greasy hair…which my mother assured me is not funny at all. How was I to know that April Fools would ruin Easter?

April Fools Day has a long and storied history. While the exact origins of April Fools are vague, most historians believe the tradition dates back to April 1st, 1582. The old Julian calendar possessed a flaw. The Julian calendar, over time, was losing days relative to the seasons. It had become so pronounced that January 1st was falling in Spring. At the Council of Trent in 1563, a new calendar, the Gregorian Calendar, was adopted which was 365 days and included a complicated leap year system which would keep the season fixed to the calendar. In 1582, the switch was made, but many people throughout Western Europe were not keen to the change. So instead of celebrating the New Year near the winter solstice on the new January 1st, they instead celebrated the new year near the vernal equinox…on April 1st. Everyone celebrating on April 1st became the butt of jokes and other hoaxes…the first April Fools Day.

Other historians say the tradition goes back to Roman times. The Romans celebrated Hilaria. Hilaria was tied to the vernal equinox around April 1st every year. The participants would dress up in disguises. This sounds like a spring time Halloween to me so I'd have to differ with the historians.

The modern April Fools Day can be traced back to the 1700's in Scotland. It was a two-day affair…my family could certainly appreciate this. On the first day, everyone would go "hunting the gawk," in which people were sent on phony errands, or fools errands. The following day was Tallic Day, where everyone would play pranks on others butts, like pinning "kick me" signs on them, or tails to their britches. This two-day April Fools might be the most notable cultural feat to come out of the Scottish Enlightenment.

The fair happens in September, not April. So what is the relevance of pranks?

The fair last for five days. We show for two days, we have the sale on Saturday morning, but we have nearly two and a half days with really nothing else going on. We do ride the rides, but nobody in my group of friends has enough money to buy a P.O.P. pass for more than one day. So we spend the rest of our time creating mischief.

It all starts with some type of harebrained idea…usually from Benny.

"Hey guys," Benny will say, "Do you wanna go fishing for fools?"

Fishing for fools is one of the easier pranks for the fair. For this one, you simply tape some fishing line to a dollar bill. You leave the dollar bill on the ground in the middle of an aisle of the barn. This prank isn't exclusive to the barn, it can be successfully performed at any high traffic area.

With the fishing line secured to the dollar bill, you place the dollar on the ground and hold onto the fishing line fifteen to twenty feet away. As the fair goers pass by, eventually one will reach down to pick up the dollar bill. And when they do, you give that fishing line a tug. Many people will catch on to the prank at this point. They will look around and see a small cadre' of kids giggling at their expense and that is the end of it.

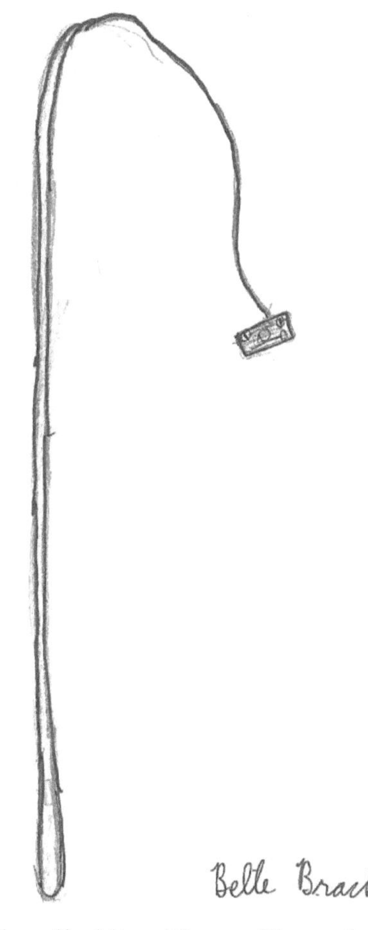

Other people will really bite. They will see the dollar bill and watch it move. They will assume it was just a breeze and jump after it. They will try to stomp on the dollar bill. This is where an experienced fisherman is needed or you will lose your dollar. The prankee will jump, dive, crawl, and shimmy after this dollar. When the dollar is safely pulled back to the fisherman, everyone in the vicinity will laugh at the poor sucker's expense.

The only problem with fishing for fools is that someone that has quick reflexes can step on the moving dollar and the prank has suddenly cost you a dollar. Or the other problem, if you pull this prank on a kid that has done this prank on someone else, they will know about the fishing line. Knowing about the fishing line, they will step on the line and the dollar will be lost. But the risk is worth it. We will spend hours watching people chase after the slippery dollar.

Another prank that we like to do works best at the beer garden. The fair is a family friendly event, but one of the sponsors is a beer distributor. The fair used to not sell beer, but the fair needs the money, so they take the sponsorship money and the beer garden is the compromise. So instead of selling beer everywhere and drunks rampaging over all of the fair, the fair has a fenced off area with a tent where all of the drunks can get their fix.

Early in the morning, before the fair really even opens, we sneak over to the beer garden and about fifteen feet, a little off the center of the entrance, we dig a one-foot-deep hole. The hole is about four inches in diameter and straight sided. We have a bucket for all of the dirt so that no evidence of the hole remains. We empty the bucket behind the pig barn and carry water to the hole with the same bucket. We mix the water around a little bit to make the water as murky as chocolate milk. If everything is done meticulously, then the hole looks like a puddle.

We leave and come back early in the afternoon. One thing we know about drunks is that they wander into the beer garden, consume adult libations, and then wander back out of the beer garden not paying any attention.

This is where our water filled hole comes in. To a person paying attention, our hole looks like a puddle…certainly to be avoided, but not an imminent danger. But the drunks stumbling out of the beer garden won't even try to avoid the puddle. They will stagger and stumble and step right into the puddle. But the puddle doesn't have a bottom and they sink down almost to their knee. Remember we mix the water so that it will be muddy and that muddy water will stick to their freshly pressed, going to town, blue jeans.

We laugh until our sides hurt. We have to stay pretty far away because if anybody found out the hole was put there on purpose, there is a good chance someone would box our ears, or tell the sheriff's deputy. So we laugh from a distance and as quietly as we can.

Eventually, we get bored, and we wander around the fair. This is where we get a second chance to enjoy our prank. Whenever we see someone walking down the midway, we will see someone walking around with a wet or muddy pant leg up to their knee. Some of them will still be wiping the mud and water off as they walk. We all stifle our laughs until we get past and then we will double over in laughter. This part of the prank can last all afternoon and into the night.

Eventually, an employee of the fair will place an orange cone next to the hole. This will stop most from falling in, but surprisingly, there will be a few that stumble in. We are always surprised that they don't just fill the dirt back in. All of the workers are super busy during the fair and we don't put the dirt in an obvious place, and maybe that's the reason.

The other thing that Benny likes to do is to harass the mascots. Benny hates mascots. Most kids will get upset or cry whenever they get next to a mascot, whether it's a guy dressed up like the Easter Bunny or someone in a Mighty Mouse costume. They are all creepy. I'm sure that Benny cried when he encountered mascots when he was younger, but his disdain for mascots has lingered longer than a normal person will admit.

Because Benny is slightly more mature than a baby, and has the ability to verbalize his fears, we can gain some insight into how younger kids react to a masked mascot.

Benny says that it's real simple. Mascots are universally creepy. They have eyes, but they don't blink, and they will talk without their lips moving. Now that Benny has pointed it out, mascots are kind of creepy.

Because of this hatred toward mascots that Benny holds in his heart, he can't help but lash out at the mascots. There are two costumed mascots that show up to the fair. Smokey Bear and the KLIX Clucker. Smokey Bear is iconic and most likely you have seen a picture of him. It is a mascot of a bear wearing a forest ranger hat, a pair of blue jeans and no shirt or shoes. I have learned that very little about a mascot makes sense, but if you're going to give him pants, shouldn't he have a shirt and shoes too. If he ever wants to go to a convenience store, he won't make it through the front door because of the whole "no shoes, no shirt, no service" policy. It's like the policy is specifically written to exclude Smokey Bear.

Another mystifying aspect of Smokey Bear is his tail. Because he's wearing pants, his tail should be covered by his pants. But Smokey has a special pair of pants that have a peep hole so his tail can poke out the back of his pants. This tail is what Benny focuses on.

As we walk down the midway, Benny spies Smokey Bear and a maniacal look is plastered across his face.

"I'm gonna get Smokey," Benny says.

I know what Benny's got planned and it makes quite a scene. Maybe I can stop him, "What did Smokey ever do to you?" I ask.

"He makes me feel like a failure," Benny replies nonsensically.

"How's that?" I ask, secretly afraid of the answer.

"Smokey says that only I can prevent forest fires."

"Yeah, that's his tag line," I say as we walk closer to Smokey. "What of it?"

"Do you remember that lightning strike in August?" Benny asks.

"Yeah," I say, not sure where this is going. "It burned over 10,000 acres."

"Ten thousand acres that Smokey is pinning on me," Benny speaks more confidently than he should. "I couldn't prevent that lightning strike, and Smokey is putting all the blame on me."

We are within yards of Smokey and there seems to be no reasoning with him. I fade back, hoping not to be implicated in Benny's crime. Smokey Bear is pretty awkward in the massive costume. He has limited view and abbreviated movement. Benny ducks in behind Smokey, grabs and yanks on his tail, and scurries away with Smokey's tail in hand. He holds it aloft like a championship trophy for ten quick strides. He then tucks it under his wing like a football and runs.

"Somebody grab that kid," I hear from the crowd.

"That kid," can be translated as "any kid," so I take that as my que to leave. I spin on my heel and start walking. I can't run or I'll look like I'm involved, which I am, indirectly.

So I walk with vigor but not haste. I can see Benny and he is running toward the campers. That seems like a good idea, so that's where I go…but I take the long way around. When I reach Benny's camper, I knock gently on the door. I can hear Benny stomping around inside, but he doesn't answer.

"Open up, Benny," I whisper loudly, "it's me."

The door flings open and Benny grabs me by the collar and pulls me in.

"Did anybody see you?" Benny asks me. Smokey's tail is already displayed prominently above the dinner table like any other hunting trophy.

"You need to change your shirt," Benny tells me.

Benny has already changed from a red T-shirt to a yellow one with a white collar. He throws a green 4-H T-shirt to me. Green really isn't my color, but it is as different as any blue shirt that I usually wear.

"You'll have to leave your hat here," Benny tells me.

Benny thinks of everything. This is actually a tried-and-true evasion tactic that every kid knows. Every kid looks the same to an adult. The only distinguishing characteristic adults use to differentiate us is the clothes we wear. So Benny and I, a kid in a yellow T-shirt and green T-shirt will walk around the midway with impunity. The Smokey Bear tenders are looking for a miscreant in a red T-shirt.

So there we are, back on the midway. Benny is a size smaller than I am, so I look like a meat head trying to show off my muscles…except I don't have any muscles.

I just like walking around, enjoying the fair, but Benny seems like he's on a mission. He walks deliberately toward the KLIX radio booth…home of the other mascot at the fair.

"Where are we headed, Benny?" I ask, afraid of the answer.

"There's one more tail I need to hang on my wall," Benny says. He is like a man possessed.

"Why, Benny?" I ask, knowing nothing could stop him.

"This scourge of mascots must come to an end," Benny replies.

When someone starts talking about ending scourges, it's best to get out of his way. As we approach the radio station booth, we hear the music and the double talk of the disk jockey followed by a broadcast echo from the state-of-the-art speakers.

For some, again, inexplicable reason, the mascot for the radio station is a giant yellow chicken…the KLIX Clucker.

It's a punny play on words. It's too cheesy to be cool, but kids and adults alike flock to the giant man-sized chicken to get their free promotional item. Some years it's a pen or a balloon. This year, it is a mechanical clicker. That's right, the KLIX Clucker is handing out clickers. In spite of the edgy alliteration, the whole thing is annoying. Thousands of kids have been given these clickers and cumulatively, it sounds like a pestilence of crickets descending upon the fair. On second thought, I might enjoy Benny yanking off his tail.

This one will be more of a challenge. The chicken costume is less bulky than the Smokey Bear and the chicken is much more agile. The chicken has two tenders and it seems like word has gotten around about Smokey's missing tail. The tenders both stand back behind the chicken.

But I have full faith that Benny can accomplish his task. Benny hesitates…I hope that he has changed his mind, but that's not Benny. There is a crowd of families descending upon the Clucker. They all want a clicker from the Clucker. It appears that Benny is using them as a distraction. Benny blends into a family of a mother and her six children. If there are six kids, it's really easy for the seventh to blend in.

Benny's group isn't interacting directly with the Clucker, which Benny planned perfectly. His group ends up directly behind the unaware man in a chicken costume. The Clucker hands out clickers and Benny grabs the Cluckers feathery tail and yanks hard toward the ground. The feathery tail ends up in Benny's hand and he immediately runs. Benny doesn't display his trophy this time, but instead scurries. This time both tenders run after Benny. He leaves a trail of yellow feathers behind him. Benny knows the most crowded parts of the fair. He runs straight to the food vendors. This is where he loses the first tender. The fact that the first one is slightly overweight and certainly out of shape is the real reason he pulls up. But the second tender is surprisingly persistent. He

is right on Benny's tail, so Benny doubles back to the Merchants Building.

The narrow aisles are always crowded, but Benny isn't able to shake the guy. He really wants that tail back. The feathers leave a trail for him to follow and Benny can't shake him. Benny takes a hard left and runs toward the livestock barn. Benny has opened up a small lead, but the persistent tender still follows.

Benny heads for this home turf…the steer barn. The steer barn is a labyrinth of aisles and corners. But everywhere Benny dodges, the tender ducks right behind. In a final act of desperation, Benny climbs the stairs to the restrooms. About halfway up there is a half door access to a balcony for utility work. The door is locked, but Benny has been exploring the fairgrounds for almost a decade now, so he knows that the access door rarely gets closed tightly. Benny opens the door, slips through, and then closes the door loosely behind him. The pursuer climbs the stairs behind Benny and runs past the service access. He runs up the second flight of stairs and into the bathroom. He searches the stalls and opens a cleaning closet.

This guy has really got is in for me, Benny thinks to himself. And I know this because this is how Benny told the story to me.

Benny pulls on the door and shakes it until it latches tightly. The pursuer runs back down the stairs and stops at the access door. He turns the knob and finds that it is locked. He pulls and pushes and sees that the door is latched. With a flummoxed look on his face, he walks down the stairs. Benny takes a deep breath, vows that his tail stealing days are over, and settles in for a long wait.

I'm a little worried that Benny got caught. I never ran, so I lost Benny about the same time as the chubby tender. I walk through the food vendors. I walk through the Merchants Building. The sheriff has a little twenty-foot by twenty-foot office that he moves into during the fair. I walk by the office to see if I can spot Benny. You know where Benny is, but I can't find him anywhere.

I walk to the campers and knock on the door. Uncle Bill answers. I'm pretty sure I woke him up from a nap, and he tells me that Benny's not in the camper.

I wander down to the steer barn. If Benny's not there, then I will hang out with T-bone. T-bone is sprawled out, laying on his side. He rolls back up to a cud chewing position when I show up. I check his water and it's untouched. T-bone lies back down on his side, so I decide to wander through the barn.

As I get to the center of the three wings that make up the steer barn, I hear a voice from above.

"Max," I hear a whispered cry for help. "Max," I hear Benny again. I look in a nearby stall, but see nothing.

"Up here, Max," Benny says in a hushed voice.

"I've been looking everywhere for you," I say as I look up, "I thought you got caught."

"Help me get down, Max," Benny says a little louder now.

"How'd you get up there?"

"You know the little door that leads to the restroom?"

"Yeah…I'm on my way."

I duck into the door that leads to the restroom. The door has a spring on it so it slams loudly behind me. I dart up the twelve, grey painted stairs to a landing. The mens room is eight more steps up to the left, the ladies room is eight steps up to the right, and in front of me is an off-white colored door with a porcelain door knob. I twist on the knob, but is doesn't move. I push on the door, but only meet resistance.

"It won't open," I tell Benny.

"There's a trick to it," Benny says, "and the trick only works from that side."

"What's the trick?" I ask.

"Pull in on the knob, twist to the left and push," Benny explains the simple procedure.

I pull, twist, and push and the door swings open. Benny stands on the loft with the Clucker's tail still in his hand.

"I thought you got caught," I tell Benny.

"I almost did…don't mess with that guy's chicken," Benny laughs.

Benny walks to a corner of the loft, lifts a loose panel and place the tail in the void behind the loose panel.

"I don't want to risk that guy seeing me with the tail," Benny says, "We'll come back for it later.

But we never did. Later that afternoon, a maintenance man drilled a hole in the wall and in the door. He then looped a chain through the holes and slapped a pad lock on the chain. It turns out that kids had figured out how to use the access door and had been horsing around on the utility loft. And it's "dangerous" for the kids to be up there, so Benny never did retrieve the tail. For all I know, it's still up there.

Saturday of the fair is always a whirlwind of activity. The day starts with the Fat Stock Sale. This is actually the culmination of the 4-H project. There are hundreds of buyers that ever pay for a fattened hog, beef, or lamb. Us kids are the beneficiary of the over payment. It's a little like show day. We have to wash and fit our steers, but there is no judging…we just walk through the sale ring. Dad says to do a good job because sale day is the most important show of the fair.

The sale treats us pretty well. T-bone brings $1.25 per pound. Do the math on that. T-bone is over 1,000 pounds. But my parents make me put the money in a savings account for college. Dad jokes and says this steer check with pay for my Math class my first semester. At least I think he's joking.

After the sale, we wash our steers one last time. It's usually hot, so it typically devolves into a water fight. It's not just squirt guns and water balloons. The wash rack has eight bays and two faucets at each bay. Almost every family has at least one 5-gallon bucket and a hose with a spray nozzle. All the faucets are wide open and being sprayed in every direction. If the winner of a water fight is the one that is driest, then no one wins and everyone loses. Everyone is dripping with water. The second part of the water fight is the mud that remains after the fight. Fortunately, I remembered to change back into my grubby clothes, which are already ruined.

Saturday night of the fair is a very predictable routine for my family. First, we hit the midway for dinner. May grandpa is a member of a barber shop choir that has a fundraising booth at the fair every year. They sell Tater Pigs and everyone in my family gets a Tater Pig. A Tater Pig is a baked potato with a hole cut in it lengthwise. A sausage is cooked and placed in the hole of the potato. You can slather it in cheese and chili, but I like my Pig with just butter and sour cream…a "naked pig" they call it.

After our Tater Pig, the whole family heads to the grandstand at the rodeo arena. For the next three hours, we watch the professional rodeo. I marvel at the skills of these ropers and riders. The whole evening is action packed and entertaining.

There is always a special act at the fair and this year, it's Monty Montana. Monty Montana does rope tricks. He will twirl his rope and the spinning and twirling ropes will do things that seem physically impossible to do. I am mesmerized throughout.

For the finale of his act, he will rope five riders. He has three rodeo queens and two pickup men run across the arena and when they reach the center of the arena, Monty Montana will throw out a massive loop and all five riders will ride safely through the loop. I'm sure this is how Monty Montana explained it to the three rodeo queens and two pickup men.

But the thrill lies in the uncertainty. The five riders line up on the north side of the arena. A hush comes over the crowd as they ride at a full gallop toward the south end of the arena. As they ride past the center, Monty Montana throws a massive 50-foot loop over all five. The hushed crowd watches as one foot of one horse inadvertently hits the rope and pulls the whole thing tight. The loose rope then turns into a trip line and all five horses trip and fall. There are cowboys and cowgirls flying in all directions. The arena is strewn with chaps, spurs, hats, crowns, rhinestones, and boots. It takes several minutes to collect all of the paraphernalia littering the arena. The normally talkative announcer is uncharacteristically silent. The crowd is hushed, waiting to cheer for the successful finale that never comes. Fortunately, the rodeo isn't over. There is still barrel racing and bull riding to save the night.

The rodeo ends and the chill of an early fall night envelops the fairgrounds. The neon lights of the carnival flash. The noise of music of every genre, kids screaming, gears turning, and a thousand conversations. The smell of roasted nuts, greasy cheese burgers, sugary treats of every kind, sawdust, straw and manure mix together in a smell unique to the fair. I drink it all in and savor the experience that is the fair, knowing that this time tomorrow, it will all be gone. But there is still several hours more of the fair.

It's well past ten o'clock. My parents rarely let me stay up past ten, much less out past ten. But it's been a long week for them too and I guess they don't have the energy to properly parent. It couldn't be that they want us to enjoy ourselves the last day of the fair.

Most of the commercial buildings are closed. The exhibits are mostly closed. Most of the animals would be asleep…if they fell asleep at night. The food vendors are closing their order windows, one by one as the orders dry up. The carnival is still very alive, but we already rode the rides. We have all been burned at least once by the carnival games.

"Pop a balloon, win a prize," the carnival barkers. I've fallen for that one.

You pay an outrageous amount of money for three darts. It doesn't matter if you pop all three balloons, the prize is considerably less than the prizes they have displayed.

"But I wanted the stuffed Mighty Mouse," you will whine, not realizing how worthless it is to argue with a carnie. Carnies don't care.

"You have to pop 1,472 balloons to win that prize," the carnival worker will say without emotion.

"So what do I win?"

"This yellow string and some pocket lint." I know it's not really yellow string and pocket lint, but it might as well be.

Really, the only entertainment left is laughing at the teenagers and their exploits. Benny, Randy, and I wander around looking for this. We see a group of about 40 teens milling about in the sheep show ring. We know something is afoot, we're just not sure what it is. After about twenty minutes, ten deputy sheriffs slowly walk up to the crowd. Like us, they are sure something is up. What they don't know is that they are part of the joke.

The deputies creep closer and move in simultaneously in four different directions. As the deputies get almost within questioning distance, one of the teenagers yells, "run."

And with that, all forty of the teenagers scatter. The deputies, now certain something is up, try grabbing as many teens as they can. When all the dust settles, the deputies are breathing heavily and obviously flustered. They begin an investigation with the teens that they hold by the collar.

"What are you kids doing?" the interrogating officer asks.

"We aren't doing anything," the teen replies with a smirk.

"Who was fighting?"

"No one was fighting."

"Who was drinking?"

"There's no alcohol."

"Then what were you doing."

At this point, the teen should have yelled, "April Fools." If they were anywhere else, they might have cited him for loitering, but this is the fair. Loitering is encouraged.

The mystified officer lets go of the smirking teen and tells him to stay out of trouble.

"Only a bunch of fools would play a prank on police officers," Benny says.

"Your brother was in there," I reply.

"He is a fool. And so are your two fool brothers."

"I like it," Randy says. He also has one fool brother in the crowd. "Did you see the look on the deputies' faces when they ran. It was great," Randy forces out a couple of chuckles just to emphasize how funny this is.

We wander back through the fair. Near the commercial building, is a spa company selling hot tubs. They have several hot tubs full of water and heated up. All week, people have been dipping their hands in the water so the salesman can prove the water is as hot as he claims. So the hot tub is a petri-dish of germs and too much chlorine.

Despite this, there are a couple of older boys and their girlfriends in their bathing suits taking an afterhours dip in the hot tub.

"Watch this," Benny says, "I've seen this happen earlier in the week."

We perch on a bench at the front of the commercial building. Close enough that we can see, but far enough away that we don't get swept up when the deputies start grabbing wayward children.

It takes longer than we hoped. We were just about to give up when three police cars pull up with lights flashing. There are flash lights shined at the trespassing soakers. The two girls look frightened and the two boys look annoyed. The four older teens step out of the hot tub.

The deputies, knowing the routine, have towels available and the youth wrap up in the towels. The deputies lead them to their car and sit them uncuffed in the back seat.

"I wonder what they're being arrested for?" Randy asks.

"Bathing in public," I respond, just guessing.

"They get 'em on trespassing," Benny replies knowingly. "They won't take them to jail, but their parents have to pick them up in their bathing suits."

Randy and I both look quizzically at Benny as if to ask, how do you know so much?

"It's the third time this week I've seen someone get busted here," Benny defends himself.

If Benny has been out this late every night, I wonder when he sleeps. Is it possible that Benny is a vampire…or maybe a steer. Steers don't sleep either. That reminds me of T-bone. I'll go check his hay and water.

T-bone rests lazily as I walk into the barn. He stands up and stretches, curling his tail and farting. That's nothing new…it would be noteworthy if he wasn't farting. As I suspect, T-bone is not sleeping. I've never seen a cow sleep, but I'm not sure. I'll ask Dad. He probably doesn't know, but he's never been afraid to posit an answer.

T-bone's water is about half full. It's probably okay until morning, but I refill it anyway. Dad says that on the range, a cow will come into the water trough and take one big drink every day. The water hole is a place where prey congregate, predators know this, so prey is very vulnerable at the water hole.

But T-bone has spent the last week with thousands of predators scoping him out without one of them eating him, so he is getting lackadaisical with all of his prey instincts. Instead of one big drink, he casually sips his chlorinated water throughout the day.

His hay bucket is similar…about half full. So I grab a couple of flakes of hay and refill his bucket. I scratch him on the tail head and he wags his tail and pins his ears back. He would let me do this all night, but I get bored with it and stop.

As I finish, my parents mosey into the barn. Mom and Dad are both carrying a child and Laney wanders behind. They stop at the tack room and Laney joins her two younger siblings in napping.

"How's the steers?" my Dad asks.

"T-bone's just fine," I reply.

"Did you check any of the others?" he inquires.

"I haven't gotten to that yet," I reply. I throw the "yet" in there to imply that I was going to, but I have no interest in the other steers.

Dad adds some water and hay to the other three steers. About the time he finishes, Jerry and Jimmy come around the corner. Their timing is impeccable.

"Did you boys find any trouble?" my Dad asks, jokingly.

"We tried to, but couldn't find any," Jerry replies. Dad laughs. I know that Jerry is answering honestly, I watched it, but I'm not going to be the one to rat him out.

"Let's head home," my Mom says. Everyone else looks tired. Mom, as usual, looks haggard.

"It's too far of a drive," my Dad says, "Let's just go to Grandma's house." I can sense Laney's eyes rolling beneath her closed eye lids. I give Dad an obligatory smile.

Before we round the corner to leave, I glance one more time at T-bone. He's chewing his cud and swats at a fly on his back. I get a kind of empty feeling in the pit of my stomach as I step out the door and leave T-bone behind.

The fair doesn't end abruptly. It kind of winds down like a spinning top. The top gets slower, wobbles a couple of times, spins a little bit more and then stops. The fair hasn't stopped, but it is most certainly wobbling.

Chapter Eleven
The End

The End...Those two little words. So hollow and empty. If you're reading a great book, you can get just a taste of the feeling. As you get to the last few pages, you know it's coming. The book usually separates it from the rest of the text, just so you won't miss it. And there it is...The End.

It's the feeling of loss, or anticipated loss. That hallow empty feeling that creeps up from the pit of your stomach and threatens to torture your soul. The end is the end, and just the beginning of the sadness.

If you were hoping for a "Charlotte's Web" type ending, you've come to the wrong place. If you're hoping that a tiny spider had been secretly communicating with T-bone and we show up Sunday morning with a spider web that says "Some steer," nope, that's not this story. This is more of an "Old Yeller" type story.

As a farm kid, I am familiar with death. We have cows, horses, dogs, cats, chickens, and all kinds of wildlife around our place. And despite our best efforts to keep everything alive, animals are dying around here all the time. And it all kinds of death. My brothers and I like to shoot ground squirrels in the spring. They die bloody and violent deaths. But I don't shed a tear for them. We constantly have barn cats coming and going. We get a litter of kittens and they grow up. And then one day, that calico cat doesn't come to the barn at feeding time. We never get proof of their demise, but their death is certain and their loss is rarely even a footnote in our life.

In the winter after weaning the calves from the cows, we will have weaned calves that will catch pneumonia. We will give them antibiotics and sulfa pills. We will put them into a special set of pens and, even with all this effort, some of these calves will die. I will watch them take their last breath and then watch Dad touch their eyeball to make sure their dead. If they're still alive, they'll blink. We don't like when it happens, but it isn't that upsetting.

We've had dogs die. We've had old dogs that will lie down and not get up so we take them to the vet to be put down. Dad always says, "I wish putting a dog down wasn't the right thing to do, but no animal is going to suffer on my watch."

And we've had dogs that die more suddenly. We had a puppy that got run over by a tractor near our house. I hardly knew the puppy, and I can't remember his name, but I cried my eyes out.

I've even watched horses die. I had a horse that became super skinny. We de-wormed him, floated his teeth and gave him special feed. But one cold night, he went to sleep and didn't wake up the next morning. It was hard to watch him wither away to a bag of bones and then just stop living, and we felt helpless about his plight.

I've even had grandparents die. In one summer, we lost both my grandma and my grandpa within a few months of each other. I didn't actually see it, Mom and Dad told me about it. I knew they were both sick and it wasn't a surprise to anyone, but it was still sad. And even sadder because of the sadness I saw from my parents and all my aunts and uncles.

But today is very different and I'm not entirely sure why. T-bone is very alive today, and I won't see him die. In fact, it will be in a facility two states away. I'm just going to put him on a truck, and then it will be over.

Sunday morning after the fair is very surreal and strangely melancholy. The fun and festive atmosphere of the night before is nearly silent. The carnival workers have spent all night tearing down the rides. All of the food booths are coming down, the tractors are driving away, and exhibitors from the produce barn carry their once vibrant, prize winning produce out of the fair. The merchants are gone, the fair is unmistakably over.

I turn the corner and there lies T-bone. He slowly chews his cud, patiently waiting for his morning feeding. We measure out the feed and place it in front of him. He wags his tail as he eats for one last time. He seems happy…as happy as a steer can be. He is actually oblivious to what's going on. That's the blessing of being prey. Your life is pretty good if you're not scared, and T-bone isn't even a little bit scared. But the curse we have as humans is an awareness of what's going on. And a range of emotions that include fear, sadness, and dread. Dread is what I'm feeling right now.

Everybody handles it differently. Jerry and Dad scurry around getting tack and leftover feed ready to take back home. I think that's a good idea. If you stay busy, it keeps your mind off the dread. But I feel like wallowing in sadness, so I sit in the hay next to T-bone.

Laney is just like all the other girls. Her eyes are puffy and she sniffles and wipes her eyes. Laney is mean to me, she's moody, and difficult to be around. But even I feel sorry for her. Her steer is laying down and chewing his cud. Laney is draped over his back and seems to not mind the child on his back. Laney's arms are wide open and her eyes water and drip tears on his back. Her steer will break her heart, but he just indifferently chews his cud.

I sit next to T-bone. He lies back down to further chew his feed. The straw is soft but it reeks of urine and manure. I want to tell T-bone something. Maybe I should tell him "I'm sorry" that I'm going to put him on the truck. Maybe I should tell him "thank you" for showing a rookie 4-Her how to care for and train a steer.

It seems silly to say anything really, so I just kneel next to him and pet his tailhead. I'm getting emotional, but T-bone just grinds on a cud that he has regurgitated and is chewing. If I could look into his brain, all I would see is, "Yummy…feed. This is really good feed."

"The truck is here," the Beef Superintendent hollers from the back of the barn.

And with that simple prompt, the barn jumps back to life. Laney is full out sobbing now. Jimmy and Jerry untie their steers. I take this unspoken que and I untie T-bone. We walk to the alley and trudge to the truck behind Jerry and Jimmy and their steers. Laney follows behind us with her steer and Dad follows us all. T-bone bucks once as we walk, but I pull on the lead rope and my well-trained steer resumes his steady walk. We reach a concrete loading chute at the back of the barn. No one talks, some kids are crying. We wait in the slow-moving line to put our steers on the truck. The line moves forward and eventually we are walking up the concrete steps. Jerry and Jimmy are right in front of me. Jerry reaches the door of the cattle hauler first. He leads his steer through the door and then returns with an empty halter a few seconds later. Jimmy is next and he repeats the process. Then it's my turn. Dad has made his way up to the top step to help me. Me, my Dad, and T-bone walk into the truck. The steers have already slung poop all over the recently cleaned truck. The truck drivers always bring a clean truck to the fair.

"I can get it," I tell my Dad. He knows that I mean I can pull the halter off of T-bone. My Dad hears me, but lingers close by, just in case.

I scratch T-bone between his shoulder blades and then grab the halter behind his ears and pull it over his head.

"Bye, T-bone," I say weakly. He lumbers to the front of the truck and starts butting heads with another steer. That thin piece of rope really is the difference between a show steer and a range steer. My Dad pats my shoulder and I walk off the truck with my empty halter.

Everything stings my eyes…the sun, the breeze, the dirt. I blink, but every time I do, my eyes just water more. I pass by Benny and Randy, but nobody says anything…there really isn't some canned, socially acceptable comment for this situation; just a communal sense of ending.

I walk quickly back to our stalls in the barn and busy myself with cleaning up. I just want to leave. I can't stop thinking about the last thing I said to T-bone. "Bye?" That's the best I can come up with for a steer that has shown me the ropes. I feel silly giving it a second thought. T-bone understands English as well as I understand Cow…or whatever the Moo language is called. But that was all I could say…"Bye?"

Dad and Laney finally walk back to the stalls. Dad has his arm around Laney and Laney is dragging her empty halter behind her. She is still crying despite Dad's comfort. Dad helps her sit down and then he comes over to me.

"Everything okay, Max," my Dad asks.

"Yeah," I say, as a tear escapes from my right eye. I've been trying not to cry. I didn't want to look like a sissy in front of my friends.

"I'm proud of you, Max," my Dad says.

That's all it takes for the tears to really flow. I feel like a bumbling boob.

"It's okay to be sad," my Dad says, "but let's not be sad alone. Let's be there together."

My Dad wraps his arm around me. I convulse and drip tears.

"We're cattlemen, Max," my Dad explains. "This is what we do. Every year I grow up a crop of calves and every year, we put them on a truck to go down to the sale. It's my least favorite part of being a cattleman, but it's all part of the job."

I look up at my Dad. I know he's trying to help, but it isn't working.

"Remember last spring when we started out?"

I nod my head between sobs.

"I told you that T-bone has eyes on the side of his head. That means that he is prey…right."

I nod again. I'm not sure where he's going with this, but I'm skeptical of his comfort.

"In that natural world, Max, that means that T-bone was designed to be a meal. Whether it's for a wolf, or a coyote, or a crow, or even for a cranky kid at McDonalds, prey is destined to be a meal. T-bone's whole purpose for being here is to be a meal. You can't ride a steer like a horse, they can't make milk, and they are too stinky and clumsy to be a pet. His magical power is to convert grass into meat. And to fulfill his purpose, we have to put him on the truck."

I know Dad is right, but it doesn't make it hurt any less. I mean, T-bone and I have been through a lot together. When I picked him out, he was a scrubby little fuzz ball. We made it through the mud of spring, the toil of halter breaking, and every day, there I was, pouring more grain into his trough. We were a team at the fair, and even to the last, there we were, side by side. And all I told him was, "Bye."

"Max, T-bone's purpose is self-evident. It is dictated by nature," my Dad says. "But our purpose gets to be a little more complicated. We can be whatever we want to be. It's our job to give our life meaning and purpose. And you should try every day to discover and fulfill your purpose." My Dad pauses, I think to let what he just said sink in. "If your purpose is to be a cattleman, then this is what you'll have to learn to do. Every fall, we put our hard grown cattle on a truck and send them down the road."

"But, Dad," I cry as I choke on what I'm about to say, "the only thing I told him was 'bye,'"

"Well, maybe 'good bye' was all you had left to say," my Dad replies.

Sometimes my Dad surprises me. I know he knows a lot about life, but he doesn't always have the answer. But sometimes, every now and then, he says something that just makes sense.

And maybe this story is more like "Charlotte's Web" after all. Except maybe T-bone is like the spider instead of the pig. He spends the summer teaching me how to be a better me. And then at the end, T-bone just fades into the story and there I am…a prize winning pig at the fair. Except I didn't win anything…and I'm not a pig.

The End

About the author...

Gus Brackett was raised on a working cattle ranch in the wide open spaces of Southwestern Idaho and Northeastern Nevada. He was on the back of a horse by the age of five and sold his first steer at the age of ten. Gus was enrolled in a one-room school house where he first started writing stories about cowboys.

As a boy, Gus listened to tall tales about early cowboys from Grandpa Noy Brackett, Uncle Rolly Patrick and Truman Clark. Gus was fascinated by these stories and started writing the Badger Thurston series in 2010 to chronicle these tales.

Gus currently lives and works on the same ranch where he was raised. He is the Chairman of the Board of the one room school where he first wrote cowboy stories. He lives in a little ranch house with his wife Kimberly, four children, and a barn full of horses, steers, dogs, cats, and chickens. He is still writing so look for other books.

If you enjoyed My Summer with T-bone, you will enjoy the other books by Gus Brackett.

It's the year 1910. Badger Thurston is an ordinary kid, but trouble seems to find him wherever he goes...as a cowboy, as a teamster, and as a flunkie on a construction site.

The Badger Thurston books will be enjoyed by the whole family. Action, adventure, mystery…these easy reading books will spark your interest in the Old West.

Badger Thurston and the Cattle Drive
Badger Thurston and the Runaway Stagecoach
Badger Thurston and the Mud Pits
Badger Thurston and the Trouble at the Rodeo
Nettie McCorkle and the Horse Race

Watch for the next book in this series.

Order your copy today at:
www.badgerthurston.com or on **Amazon.com**.

Or send a check or money order for $10.25 plus $3.50 for shipping and handling to:

12 Baskets Book Publishing
54899 Crawfish Rd.
Rogerson ID 83302

www.ingramcontent.com/pod-product-compliance
Lightning Source LLC
Chambersburg PA
CBHW061427160726
47995CB00003B/790